THEORY IN PRACTICE

Tocqueville's New Science of Politics

Saguiv A. Hadari

THEORY IN PRACTICE
Tocqueville's New Science
of Politics

STANFORD UNIVERSITY PRESS 1989

Stanford, California

Stanford University Press, Stanford, California
© 1989 by the Board of Trustees of the Leland Stanford Junior University
Printed in the United States of America

CIP data appear at the end of the book

PREFACE

Our habit is to judge academic treatises by abstract and supposedly universal criteria, and indeed an author generally measures the success of his or her work by the extent to which it withstands such challenges. Nevertheless, in retrospect we also look at a piece of work as a reflection of the life of the writer. In what it does or does not address, in its tacit implications, and in its tone, a living voice comes through. My husband Saguiv Hadari began his book on Tocqueville in the bloom of youth, as a vibrant scholar and robust young man in his late twenties. He completed it in the last year of his life at the age of 32. Because of his untimely death, certain qualities of his life appear more clearly in his writing than they might otherwise have done. The style of presentation and development of arguments reflect the way he lived until the moment of his death: direct, full of wit, sure of himself with a sometimes brash energy, but tempered with a deep caring and moral approach to the world.

These characteristics coupled with his wide-ranging interests and intellectual capacities led him to the nonsectarian and democratic conclusions of his book. The content of this book, as well as his fascination with Rousseau and his developing interest in the problem of the conflict of values, all reflect a deep and persistent concern with what he termed the "limits of reason" (as he had entitled one of his courses). What are the sources of human motivation? How can we offer a fuller understanding of reason that could account for our complexity and yet provide some clarity in the face of moral dilemmas? Saguiv sought both explanation and grounds for commitment. I believe it was his strength of character, his moral courage, and not just the sharp and inclusive nature of his mind, that directed him into contested areas, places not occupied by various intellectual schools. He was not afraid to go out into the open alone.

Saguiv began work on this manuscript at Wake Forest University. From the beginning the university was supportive in every way possible, including the provision of research funding in the summers of 1984 and 1985. I thank both the university and the Politics Department for their warm and unstinting assistance over the four years Saguiv taught there. In particular, Elide Vargas provided her excellent and immediate services whenever called upon. Donald Schoonmaker, as friend and colleague, read the entire manuscript and suggested important comparative perspectives. He was also an essential and unfailing support in countless other ways.

Over this past year at Stanford University we have benefited greatly from the assistance of both the faculty and the staff of the Political Science Department, who made us feel at home here so quickly. I owe special thanks to John Ferejohn, who not only read the whole manuscript and offered suggestions but was encouraging to Saguiv throughout the year. In addition, I am most grateful to Grant Barnes of Stanford University Press for his enthusiastic and expeditious support that enabled the manuscript to be reviewed and accepted without delay. To the Press's outside readers, Terence Ball and Russell Hardin, I am also greatly indebted for their immediate response in reviewing the work, as well as for their insightful comments. The Press's attention to this matter of time gave

Saguiv a wonderful gift—knowledge that his work would be published.

I would also like to thank Jack Knight for his comments and criticisms, and George Riley for his incisive editorial work and his untiring and more than generous help in finalizing the manuscript. They and many other friends and colleagues have provided moral support in less immediate ways. Specifically, I mention with so much gratitude Hughes Evans, Larry George, Nina Halpern, Nahum Melumad, Joshua Miller, Mary Odem, and Gershon Schatzberg. I am painfully aware of those whom I have not named explicitly and hope they know how much we relied on their friendship as well. Finally, the tremendous love and assistance of our families made these years not only bearable but full of hope and pleasure.

Stanford, California   Ingrid Creppell
August 1988

CONTENTS

BIBLIOGRAPHIC NOTE

The broader aim of this work justifies a reliance on the most widely available English translations of Tocqueville's work whenever possible; Tocqueville scholars will have little trouble retracing the original. The editions used are listed below in chronological order; quotations will be accompanied by page numbers referring to these editions.

The Old Regime and the French Revolution [AR]. New York: Doubleday, 1955.
Democracy in America [DA]. New York: Doubleday, 1969.
Recollections [R]. London: MacDonald, 1970.
Selected Letters on Politics and Society [SL]. Berkeley: University of California Press, 1985.

All other translations of French originals are the author's. References to the French originals are from:

Oeuvres complètes [OC], ed. J. P. Meyer. Paris: Gallimard, 1851–.
Nouvelle correspondance entièrement inédite, VII of *Oeuvres*, [NC], ed. Gustave de Beaumont. Paris, 1866.

THEORY IN PRACTICE

Tocqueville's New Science of Politics

CHAPTER I

Introduction

To begin defining the goals of this work, it will be helpful to proceed by elimination. Though the title alludes to the fascinating mixture in Alexis de Tocqueville of theoretician and man of action, the interaction between these two realms will not be the center of attention. Tocqueville's short stint as a foreign minister and his two tenures as a deputy do make him a more interesting, complex figure, and unquestionably contributed to the richness of his thought; intellectual biography, however, is not my subject.[1] Neither will a thematic analysis be undertaken. (Most of the scholarship on Tocqueville fits under the latter rubric: for a range of statements see Aron, 1968; Birnbaum, 1970; Drescher, 1964, 1968a; Lively, 1962; Manent, 1982; Zeitlin, 1971; Zetterbaum, 1967.) Only indirectly will the substance of Tocqueville's writings be of any concern to this inquiry. In particular, the peculiar compulsion to establish batting averages, measuring Tocqueville's alleged prophecies against present-day realities, will not be indulged.[2]

[1] A number of good intellectual biographies are available: for a work covering the period of Democracy in America, see Schleifer (1980); for one on The Old Regime and the French Revolution, see Herr (1962); Gargan (1955) concentrates on the years reflected upon in the Recollections; Mayer (1966) still offers the classic overview, now superseded by Jardin's (1984) more thorough work.

[2] Though he boldly ventured broad political forecasts, Tocqueville denied the possibility of specific historical predictions and often admitted to be puzzled by the shape and pace of events.

Indeed, it deserves mention here solely for its symptomatic character: aside from revealing a simplistic conception of the task of social theory[3] (and, since Tocqueville did not share it, a misreading of his intentions), this statistical fad testifies to the most perplexing character of Tocqueville's work—its amazing endurance. Written a century and a half ago about the most rapidly changing society in history, *Democracy in America* still offers the best introduction to American—indeed to democratic—politics and culture. Similarly, despite the unparalleled relentlessness of scholarship on its subject, Tocqueville's (unfinished) *The Old Regime and the French Revolution* remains unsurpassed. In addition, notwithstanding these considerable accomplishments, aficionados consider Tocqueville's neglected *Recollections* his finest book. (See, for example, Mayer, 1966, 661; Salomon, 1935, 425.)

Precisely that perplexing endurance, so rare in modern social theorists, motivates this inquiry. The question it aims to answer is: How did his thought achieve such "conceptual robustness," how did his writings attain that "classic" status? Disregarding irreplicable factors such as personal genius and sociological circumstances, Tocqueville's method is thus the issue. Let it be clear, though, that this definition of focus should not be taken to imply the assumption of a strict separation between substantive and methodological issues. The latter, insofar as they dictate, at a higher level of abstraction, an identification of "actors" as well as an attribution of responsibility, are always also substantive. Adjusting one's focus to nations, classes, or individuals and singling out causal, structural, or intentional determinations for action surely entail substantive consequences for an analysis. Tocqueville himself, as will be shown, was sensitive to these implications. Unfortunately, his explicitness on this specific issue remains

---

[3] The term "social theory" is intended generically. Disciplinary boundaries between the various social sciences are acknowledged, albeit deemed arbitrary and unfortunate and denied ontological significance. For a similar use, see Giddens (1982, 5).

uncharacteristic: Tocqueville's habitual reticence on methodological questions will necessitate a patient, and at times inevitably imaginative, reconstructive effort.

An examination of this sort has not been made before.
The small number of short studies on Tocqueville's method
presently available, aside from their limited range, address a
different set of issues. These earlier efforts center either on
Tocqueville's specific deductive algorithms (e.g. Smelser, 1971;
Stinchcombe, 1978, chapter on Tocqueville and Trotsky) or on
the wider existential parameters grounding his approach (e.g.
Salomon, 1939; Furet, 1984). This study will be pitched at a
mid-level of abstraction between these two extremes. While
existential moorings and particular techniques certainly will
be considered, the main issues addressed will be Tocqueville's
use of abstract, formal models, his reliance on historical, hermeneutic inquiry, and the normative stand of his analyses.
A study of these essential elements of Tocqueville's method
should constitute an important contribution to the understanding of his thought, hence to social theory as a whole.

However, a still wider goal informs this inquiry. Reflecting
on the poverty of current theory (of which I am most particularly aware in my field of specialization, political theory),
I hope that a promising methodological model might be ex-
tracted from Tocqueville's immensely successful practice. In
that sense Tocqueville's call for "a new science of politics for
a brand new world," quoted in the subtitle, will be heeded.
No doubt Tocqueville meant it in a substantive way, realizing
that, with modern mass democracy, social theory was confronting a new phenomenon. That awareness, the turn toward
America as truly a New World (not merely an older, original one), the consequent struggle with language to mold new
words (e.g. "individualism")—all make Tocqueville our contemporary. His unique accomplishments in conceptualizing
modernity, for which Dilthey compared him to Aristotle and
Machiavelli, make him worthy of emulation (Dilthey, 1921,
104; quoted in Mayer, 1966, 13). Yet the focus here will be

methodological, an interpretive twist on Tocqueville's call for which the nineteenth-century expert on the matter, a friend, admirer, and critic of Tocqueville, created the precedent: "The importance of M. de Tocqueville's speculations is not to be estimated by the opinions which he has adopted, be these true or false. The value of his work is less in the conclusions, than in the mode of arriving at them" (Mill, 1961, vii). John Stuart Mill's judgment justifies turning to Tocqueville with the hope expressed earlier. Thus, in all fairness, this inquiry intends to treat Tocqueville the way he treated America, similarly mining its subject for a broader, theoretical model.

Surely such an approach is preferable to the conventional elaboration of a methodological treatise: little credence would be given to the unripe wisdom of a young scholar, as opposed to the interpretation, however liberal, of a mature, time-proven theoretical practice. Moreover, showing by doing must be reckoned a didactic technique superior to the dry precepting typical of methodological textbooks. Anchored in Tocqueville's works, through detailed case studies and countless examples, this monograph truly will depict "theory in practice." Above and beyond such personal and didactic reasons, however, this prudent approach to methodology proves more theoretically defensible. Conventional methodological discourse adopts a stance of superiority toward practice: its procedural prescriptions purport to validate or disqualify the theorist's work, a claim legitimated by an appeal either to epistemology, or to ontology, or to both. The methodologist thus allegedly possesses a privileged insight into the nature of reality, at least insofar as distinction and relation between "subject" and "object," "participant" and "observer" are concerned. Clearly, for fear of circularity, this original insight providing the preconditions for knowledge cannot be validated itself by further inquiry. Hence the dictatorial pretensions of conventional methodology seem unfounded. (See Hindess, 1977, for an elaboration of this critique, and Gunnell, 1986, for its application to political theory in particular.) Accordingly, it remains safer to assume a subordinate stance to theoretical practice and avoid " 'higher methodology'—that bourne from which no traveller returns" (Barry, 1978, 166).

Having stated this wider aspiration of providing a methodological model for social theory, I should say more about its grounds. Given this broader goal, the incompleteness of past scholarship, the twin recommendations of Dilthey and Mill, and even the remarkable endurance of his insights might not suffice to explain the choice of Tocqueville as a subject. One additional, immediate reason will be obvious. The numerous expressions of filial piety from various branches of social theory attest, in their very partiality, to the ecumenical, interdisciplinary reach of his approach.[4] Our anachronistic wonder at this feat, however, tells more about modern impoverished conceptions of theory than about Tocqueville's particular achievement: writing at that privileged moment when the nascent social science had not yet split and hardened into arbitrarily severed disciplines, Tocqueville's response to social reality as a unified whole was natural. The vital need to recapture this breadth of outlook, a reconstitution without which our considerable gains from disciplinary specialization necessarily remain meaningless, will be presumed: no need to advertise so trivial an insight.

A more fundamental lesson can be learned from Tocqueville: his theoretical practice transcends our most entrenched methodological distinctions. That successful eclecticism deserves a close examination. Drawing on two well-known organizing dichotomies, Tocqueville's approach qualifies as both "economic" and "sociological," and fuses together "classical" and "modern" theoretical perspectives. As each of these two

---

[4] For anthropology, see Dumont (1970a); for comparative politics, Bendix (1964); for comparative historical analysis, Skocpol (1979); for history, Furet (1981); for political philosophy, Zetterbaum (1972); for political theory, Lipset (1963); for the study of public opinion, Noelle-Neumann (1984); for sociology, Aron (1968); for sociology of knowledge, Mannheim (1953).

pivotal junctures bridges more than one set of seemingly opposed methodologies, I will sketch each separately, before presenting a tentative summary statement of the method.
Tocqueville's first series of transgressions unites five couples
of methodological goals and approaches now entangled in
fierce epistemological and ontological disputes, and widely believed to be irreconcilable.

(1) As even the previous allusions to *Democracy in America*
illustrate, Tocqueville's work qualifies simultaneously as no-
mologic and ideographic. That is, the absolute contrast between the quest for general laws on the one hand and immersion in particularity on the other stands refuted: Tocqueville
clearly engages in the latter, to better reach the former. No
unwarranted leap links the two, because in the process the
terms of the quest are redefined: Tocqueville's "general laws"
always remain cautiously limited in scope, and retain sufficient
flexibility for subsequent contextual applications.

(2) Competing explanatory modes are combined. Tocqueville refuses to grant priority to either causal or intentional
explanations for human conduct. His impartiality in that regard stems from a recognition of their equal validity, and his
choices alternate according to the situation and type of action
analyzed. Specific social structures determine overall patterns
of behavior, yet the intelligibility of an individual act ultimately depends on a grasp of the actor's intentions.

(3) Accordingly, the rift between formal and interpretive
approaches is healed. Though, at least by current standards, Tocqueville's formal models remain mostly implicit,
they can easily be lifted out of his text and translated into
more abstract terms. However, their embeddedness in carefully
circumscribed contexts directly expresses Tocqueville's interpretive sensitivity. Assumptions about "preferences," and
"rationality" (to borrow from one language), can be tentatively
formulated and cogently applied only within a previously deciphered cultural "horizon" (to revert to the other).

(4) Thus Tocqueville's theoretical practice resolves the al-

legedly intractable dispute between positivism and hermeneutics: by including elements of each, it equally disowns both.
Unavoidably some "data" gain the status of "facts," and broad
statistical correlations are deduced. Yet the irreducible opacity
of interpretations, at both ends of the inquiry—observer and
observed—is affirmed, indeed granted a major role in the un-
folding of history: epistemological indeterminacy is the theoretical counterpart (and guarantor) of free will and openness
to change. Accordingly, all "predictions" remain tentative, in
recognition of the crucial import of these "habits of the heart"
Tocqueville termed mores. (This caveat has too often been
neglected, making Tocqueville's "prophecies" his blessing—
when successful—and his bane—when not.)

(5) Finally, Tocqueville's theoretical practice attempts a
continual back and forth between micro- and macro- levels of
analysis. The complex blend of approaches delineated above
provides the key for this desirable but elusive translation. The
methodological individualism of the formal models balances
the holism of cultural interpretations; conversely, particular
idiosyncrasies drawn from ideographic study restitute specific
content to the abstract nomological deductions from these
models.

Rather than laboriously recapitulating these five points, we
can take a convenient shortcut through Brian Barry's characterization of the "economic" and "sociological" approaches to
social theory: "One type is axiomatic, economic, mechanical,
mathematical; the other is discursive, sociological, organismic, literary" (1978, 3). Excepting the mathematical aspect,
Tocqueville's method incorporates both approaches, offering
what Barry in the speculative mood of his book's last pages envisioned as "a package embodying the best of both" (p. 180).

Tocqueville's second series of transgressions bypasses two
allegedly insurmountable philosophical obstacles.

(1) The artificial divorce between descriptive and normative
analysis is disregarded. Not only do Tocqueville's inquiries,
like any other, secrete some implicit values; Tocqueville explic-

itly adopts a normative stand, states a commitment to openly advocated values, and passes judgment accordingly. Unsurprisingly, his work has been classified as both "political philosophy" and "social theory."

(2) Nevertheless, Tocqueville's conclusions are not simply subjective evaluations. In fact, he transcends the obstinate dichotomy of "objectivity" versus "subjectivity," as a result of his ceaseless efforts to make his assumptions explicit, to provide for alternative ones, and to refrain from absolute conclusions. Much can be learned from his reflexive awareness and the methodological strategies he employs to avoid the pitfalls of either objectivist or subjectivist extremes.

The last two points can be conveniently joined using Jürgen Habermas's shorthand categories of the "classical" and "modern" approaches to social theory. Ancient political philosophy, according to him, conceived itself as a continuation of ethics, an effort to develop prudence through the formation of character; modern social science, in contrast, stands apart from moral valuations, striving to achieve an objective knowledge to ground a stable and efficient organization of society (1973, 42–43). Tocqueville's recombination of these two stands successfully addresses Habermas's ultimate query: "How can the promise of practical politics—namely, of providing practical orientation about what is right and just in a given situation—be redeemed without relinquishing . . . the rigor of scientific knowledge?" (1973, 44).

This schematic description of Tocqueville's method will seem widely implausible to some—especially in light of this last concluding claim—and plain common sense to others. The metaphysically inclined may balk at the apparent disregard of foundational epistemological disputes, while the pragmatically oriented will presume Tocqueville's eclecticism to be commonplace. This study will endeavor to demonstrate both the coherence of Tocqueville's approach and its intricacy. A cogent conceptualization of the nature of reality and theory informs Tocqueville, and its dictates make for a complex, demanding theoretical practice. For the moment, however, the preceding sketchy elaboration of claims will have to do, as only a study of the size contemplated could make good on such promises. As a last step before plunging headlong, the structure of the monograph should be explained.

The structure of the argument flows from the themes just introduced. Its three parts elaborate on the pivotal junctures mentioned, each part building on the one preceding it to reconstruct gradually Tocqueville's method. I begin by discussing Tocqueville's use of formal models (Part I), then incorporate his reliance on hermeneutical inquiry (Part II), before addressing the issue of his normative stand (Part III). Thus step by step, the "economic" strand of Tocqueville's approach, its "sociological" component, and its mixture of the "classical" and "modern" attitudes toward social theory will be examined. The conclusion will pull together these three strands, restoring the unity of Tocqueville's method and setting it as a model for social theory. This cumulative structure eases the presentation, while forcing an equally sustained attention to each element of Tocqueville's approach. Note, however, that it calls for a patient and cautious reading: not until the last chapter can Tocqueville's method as a whole be judged.

Each part will have two chapters: a case study, focusing on the particular issue addressed in that part in the context of a specific text, and a more theoretical chapter, generalizing the findings first to Tocqueville's work as a whole and then to method in social theory in general. Case studies have been chosen so as to cover Tocqueville's main works, their order being determined by purely rhetorical considerations. To identify formal models in Tocqueville's personal *Recollections*, and study his normative stand as expressed in his magnum opus, *Democracy in America*, seemed the most striking strategy. I proceed from the most neglected to the best-known texts. Thus a reversed chronological order resulted: *Recollections*,

The Old Regime and the French Revolution, Democracy in America. Once more, especially in reading these case studies, the reader should remember that they necessarily target but one artificial "third" of Tocqueville's method, in complete isolation from the other two. Only the concluding chapter will illustrate their combination in Tocqueville's practice.

PART I

FORMAL MODELS

CHAPTER 2

Tocqueville's Formal Models: The *Recollections* Reexamined

The following reading of Part I of Tocqueville's *Recollections* is offered in an effort to illustrate one important element of his method: his use of formal models. Thus a double challenge to the conventional image of Tocqueville is posed. I contend that a great many of his analyses are grounded in abstract, nomological models of behavior, though the latter remain understated and discursively described (as opposed to a symbolic, logical, or mathematical presentation). Like any great writer, Tocqueville seeks to eliminate the scaffolding of his deductions. I further propose to uncover examples of this approach in Tocqueville's most personal and seemingly least theoretical great work. Beginning with this most neglected source, we find embedded in personal details the tools of abstract political analysis. To cite but one instance of conventional scholarly wisdom, Albert Salomon declares the *Recollections* to be Tocqueville's most beautiful book (1935, 425), yet views him as radically opposed to any application of scientific and mathematical methods to the study of politics (1939, 406).

Contrary to this widely accepted view, it will be argued that the first five chapters of the *Recollections* constitute, among other things, a study of the unintended consequences of political action: they present, admittedly in an implicit fashion, three models of such effects and explain their mechanisms.

Vindicating this claim will entail a characterization of Tocqueville, at least insofar as the text examined is concerned, as an "economist" in his approach to social theory. Quoting Barry's descriptions once more, such an approach is "axiomatic, economic, mechanical, mathematical" (1978, 3). While no trace of formal language will be found in these pages, at issue is Tocqueville's reliance on reductive models of social interaction in the effort to deduce broad nomological conclusions.

Admittedly, these seldom studied pages are written in a spontaneous and informal style. At the outset, declaring himself unable for reasons of health to pursue sustained reflection, Tocqueville resolves to engage in transcribing his reminiscences as "a mental relaxation for myself and not a work of literature" (R, 3). As this authorial statement of intent strengthens the editorial introductory comments, the reader, convinced that Tocqueville "deliberately wrote political memoirs, nothing else" (R, xii), lightly proceeds to enjoy what must be reckoned one of the most engrossing, intimate historical accounts of political life.

Yet, in any memoirs, highly elaborated vows of secrecy and privacy unwittingly testify to a concern with future public consumption. Surely Tocqueville's numerous variations and careful excisions betray not merely an awareness of a potential audience, but a desire to manipulate its judgment on the author (see R, 66n5) as well as the events described (Jardin, 1984, 429–30). Moreover, his first criterion for determining the span of memory to be tapped—the second will be examined in time —expresses the broad interest of a theorist rather than the care for minute details of a *raconteur*: the period chosen ensures that the events to be reported "had something of greatness in them" (R, 4).

Once the suspicion has been raised that Tocqueville, by design, by nature, or both, wrote as a social theorist, the pace of the reading slows down, allowing other aspects of the text's landscape to emerge. In particular, the endings of the five chapters constituting the first part assume a new prominence: these paragraphs, by which Tocqueville probably concluded successive stages of writing, and after which the common reader temporarily interrupts the reading, clearly form a thematic chain of road signs guiding a more attentive approach. Suffice it to reveal here that all five passages, obviously deserving of further interpretation, call attention to a fascinating characteristic of political action—its frequently unintended consequences.

A short digression on the meaning and use of the technical notion of "unintended consequences" is in order. Let loose in a social context, human actions seem to assume a life of their own, leading to results possibly far removed from the actors' initial intentions. Often no simple mistake of judgment or error of calculation carries the blame, but rather the complex and at times unpredictable interplay of social factors, generating positive or negative consequences, in addition to or instead of the intended objectives.[1] This phenomenon, once one learns to recognize it under various descriptions and labels, has constituted a focal point of attention for an impressive array of major theorists.[2]

Chapters 1 and 2: Introducing the Problem

The temporal setting of the first five chapters, the unexpected revolution of February 1848, provides a most conducive background for the emergence of such effects. When the habitual interaction between actors playing their normal social roles abruptly gives way to an unstructured interdepen-

---

[1] I am here following the sociologist Raymond Boudon (1979) rather than Jon Elster (one of the few political theorists recently to explore what he terms "social contradictions"), who restricts the notion to instances of strict counterfinality (1978, 109).

[2] I will further elaborate on this notion and its history in the next, more theoretical, chapter. In Tocqueville's case, Sasha R. Weitman recognized that *The Old Regime and the French Revolution* presents the French Revolution as an unintended consequence of the Ancient Regime's policies. However, his observation, coming as the last sentence in his article, remained merely a suggestion (1966, 406). Richard Vernon (1979), in writing on unintended consequences, mentioned Tocqueville explicitly; yet he not only restricted the latter's use of the concept, but also wished to limit the theoretical reach of the concept itself.

dence between agents coping with a chaotic political situation, the probability for unintended consequences of political action sharply rises (Boudon, 1979, 96–97). In such a setting, even the best political commentator is likely to fail in predicting the march of the political events and their repercussions. (See Bertrand de Jouvenel, 1965, 37, who offers precisely this historical junction—February 1848—as an example of the predictable failure of political predictions.) Thus Tocqueville himself, often celebrated for his acute prophetic vision, here admits and emphasizes the inherent limitations on prospective political judgment (e.g. R, 66) rather than, as an interpretation unaware of the peculiar theme of these chapters would conclude, the acumen of his predictions (R, xii, Mayer's introduction. Similar disclaimers on the part of Tocqueville can be found in *Democracy in America*, as Zetterbaum notes, 1967, 9).

Indeed the first chapter introduces the fascinating problem of the inherent limitations on prospective political judgment. Tocqueville's opening analysis unfolds, retrospectively, the best prospective view on the eve of the Revolution. All the threatening underlying trends are succinctly and masterfully presented: the continuing spirit of 1789 (R, 5); the mediocre materialism of the ruling middle class (R, 6); the shrinking of the public sphere, stifling political life (R, 10), and its reappearance at the bottom of society (R, 11), redirected against the last bastion of inequality—private property (R, 12); and the overcentralization retained following the relative democratization. Yet, after quoting proudly and at length from his fateful warning speech in the Assembly, Tocqueville concludes the chapter by stating he "did not expect such a revolution," and "did not see the accidents" that toppled the July Monarchy in advance (R, 16, 17). (Gargan, 1955, 58, notes that the rhetoric of that famous speech merely suggests possibilities without expressing prescient expectations; see also Lively, 1962, 124–25.) Together with this unabashed admission of lack of foresight, an important theoretical distinction is introduced between discernible "general causes" and unpredictable "accidents." I shall return to this distinction in the conclusion of this chapter.

Chapter 2 provides an explanation for the limitations on prospective political judgment, and in so doing announces the theme of the first part as a whole. Its concluding paragraph, carefully if hesitatingly placed immediately before the account of the revolution itself (R, 28, marginal note), deserves to be quoted in full: "One has to have spent long years in the whirlwind of party politics to realize how far men drive each other from their intended courses, and how the world's fate is moved by their efforts, but often in opposite directions from the wishes of those who produced the current, like a kite which flies by the opposing action of the wind and the string" (R, 28). The metaphor of the kite ironically undermines the illusory pretense of intentionality. Its tense string, boldly pointing toward the sky, proves but a thin rationalization, at best a secondary parameter, incapable of dictating the direction of the action, indeed incapable of forcing it to take flight on its own—thus utterly dependent on the capricious wind representing the effects of human plurality. (Gargan, 1963, 341, mentions this crucial metaphor, without much elaboration.) This metaphor captures the contribution of a rich political experience to a fertile theoretical mind: the insight achieved, through practice combined with reflection, into the effect of interdependence on political action. As an active political figure, Tocqueville's proximity to the political scene enabled him to ascertain the intentions of major political agents—apart from official declarations or subsequent rationalizations—and thus to testify to their frequent unanticipated frustration. From the perspective of this reading such is the crucial import of Tocqueville's second criterion for determining the span of his account, the fact that his position during the period chosen enabled him to see the events clearly (R, 4, also 125).

Chapter 3: "Overshooting"

Though the kite of political action can fly in all directions, to examine fruitfully the phenomenon of unintended consequences one must formalize its effect in better defined models. Following these two introductory chapters, each of the remaining three presents a specific effect, initially categorized by the direction of the results vis-à-vis the intentions. Chapter 3 offers an example of "overshooting," where interdependence leads to exaggeratedly magnified consequences; Chapter 5 concludes with a mirror-image example of "undershooting," where interdependence produces muted results; Chapter 4 links these two with an example of a "boomerang" effect, where interdependence generates an unexpected backlash. Although none of these unintended consequences can be dismissed as merely the upshot of superficial policy mistakes, Tocqueville shows the mechanism governing the phenomena of amplification and attenuation to be solely—if strikingly— the effect of aggregation. The examination of the case of reversal, though less elegant structurally, points to a recurrent strategic problem as well.

In the penultimate paragraph of Chapter 3 (the short concluding one once more puzzling over the author's undisturbed sleep on the eve of the unexpected revolution), Tocqueville draws again on the wind metaphor: "Those who claim to be originators and leaders of these revolutions do not originate or lead anything; their sole merit is identical with that of the adventurers who have discovered most of the unknown lands, namely the courage to go straight ahead while the wind blows" (R, 35). As a politician, Tocqueville wishes to repudiate claims to planning and calculation of the opposition's leaders: "Those who boast of conspiracies have done no more than taken advantage" of the mob's emotions (R, 35). As a theorist, however, Tocqueville aims to refute predictable historical reconstructions: "It is a waste of time to seek secret conspiracies that bring about such events" (R, 35).[3] These two critical efforts converge and coalesce into one persistent theme, announced in the passage quoted above: the impotence and lack of control of the alleged leaders. Chapter 4 resumes treatment of this theme and ends with a threatening portrait of a working-class revolutionary, mockingly voicing the movement's goals, by now far beyond all the "leaders'" expectations. Chapter 5 concludes the whole first part with a tragic if ironic summation of this theme: "So of the four men most responsible for the events of the 24th February—Louis-Philippe, M. Guizot, M. Thiers and M. Barrot—the two former were exiles by the end of the day, and the two latter were half-mad" (R, 58).

Yet despite the marked emphasis on the discrepancy between the opposition leaders' intentions and the revolutionary developments, this conclusion explicitly refuses to renounce an attribution of responsibility to the political agents. The frustration of intentionality does not snap the thread of causality connecting actions and subsequent repercussions. A later passage in Part II mentions as the first "accident" that brought about the revolution "the clumsy passions of the dynastic opposition, which prepared the ground for a riot when it wanted a reform" (R, 63). The events corroborating this accusation are reported in Part I, particularly in the account of the affair of the banquets, in which the opposition's already inflated rhetoric (R, 16) assumed passionate and inflammatory tones (R, 25, 26). This led some of the radical public to draft a truly revolutionary program for the last banquet, which in turn provoked a strong reaction from the government (R, 27). At this juncture the opposition coalition had little choice but to follow suit. The *dynastic* opposition, wary of offending its sup-

---

[3] Pierre Birnbaum rightly praises Tocqueville for his firm rejection, unusual at the time, of conspiracy theories of revolution (1970, 88); Tocqueville's critical review of Abbot Barruel's memoirs in a letter to Circourt, dated June 14, 1852, further elaborates his position (OC, XVIII, 75–76).

porters, accused the ministers of violating the Constitution, thus leading to their impeachment and unwittingly providing a ready excuse for a recourse to arms. The *radical* opposition, which "considered a Revolution premature and did not want one," nevertheless felt obliged to maintain a still more extreme stand and "fan the flames of insurrection," for fear of disappointing their now aroused followers and of losing any distinctive character in comparison with their allies from the dynastic party (R, 27). As for the program itself, "incredible though it may seem, this programme, which instantly turned the banquet into a rebellion, was composed, approved and published without the help and against the will of the parliamentarians who imagined that they still led the movement they had created" (R, 27).

Tocqueville's description documents how the unintended snowball effect that turned a parliamentary dispute into a full-fledged revolution was the result of inflated revolutionary rhetoric spreading to the masses (witness the crucial role of the press; R, 26) fueling true revolutionary ardor. (Jouvenel, 1965, agrees that affective attitudes are the key to such rapid changes.) The stunning and unexpected macrophenomenon of revolution is explained simply by the aggregation of micro-behaviors of political agents, an intelligible yet unpredictable and uncontrollable effect. One might think by analogy of the effect of one paranoid customer withdrawing large amounts of savings, and the possibly false rumor of financial instability thus generated spreading exponentially, motivating a devastating run on the bank. Indeed "overshooting" in the case of the February Revolution as well seems the vindication of a "self-fulfilling prophecy" (Merton, 1948; Buck, 1963; Henshel, 1982), the repeated exaggerated warning of an imminent collapse of the Monarchy (R, 16) finally leading to a popular rebellion. As Tocqueville makes clear, though the opposition's "adventurers" ultimately reached "unknown lands," they unintentionally launched the voyage, indeed unwittingly raised the wind by the clamor of their own voices.

Chapter 4: "Boomerang"

While the "overshooting" theme continues to dominate Tocqueville's analyses (see R, 36, on the rumor's influence), a secondary strand is woven into the description of the revolutionary developments. Dealing this time with the government's leaders and their main decision as to a strategy for controlling the insurrection, Chapter 4 offers a tight formulation telescoping their choice and its result in one short sentence: "They took the opposite course to that of the government of the elder branch, and reached the same result" (R, 37).

Clearly in this case the consequences were counterproductive. Remembering their own success in overcoming the army's resistance in 1830 and their luck in not having to confront the popular National Guard, the leaders opted not to repeat their elders' mistake and adopted a plan "to withdraw all the troops and flood Paris with national guards" (R, 37). The latter, however, as Tocqueville hastens to report (R, 40–41), were not eager to rescue the government. Indeed, the National Guard blamed the government for the problems and joined in with its detractors.

Evidently, the far-reaching consequences of the "overshooting" effect are exhibited here. Even the class represented and supported by the government—the middle class—turns against it, not from sheer material interest but from "vanity," from the pleasure in joining with everybody else in decrying and abusing the authorities (R, 41). Yet Tocqueville the theorist does not intend to dismiss the government's decision as mere folly or inexcusable ignorance. Rather, his interpretation points to a more fundamental error, one perhaps at times unavoidable in politics: "I have always noted in politics how often men are ruined by having too good a memory" (R, 37). In the daily confrontation with the need for prospective judgment, especially in times of crisis and social disorder, politicians are forced back on their past experience, and naturally draw on old patterns of action. Such of course was the char-

acter of the government leaders' decision. Founded on their
personal revolutionary experience, when implemented in the
new revolutionary context, it produced a "boomerang" effect:
"For it is very true that, although humanity is always the same,
people's outlooks and the incidents that make history vary
constantly. One time will never fit neatly into another, and
the old pictures we force into new frames always look out of
place" (R, 37).[4]

Unintended consequences in this case are not straightforwardly the result of a mechanism of aggregation, merely
marginally insofar as the National Guards' attitude can be
construed as an extreme side effect of the "overshooting" phenomenon. Moreover, the effects in this case have no predetermined direction. The unhappy yet predictable fallback on in-
applicable "lessons from the past" (see May 1973) might lead
to a variety of forms of frustration—reinforcement, attenuation, or reversal of the intended result—or even to fortuitous
successes—by unplanned routes or for unanticipated reasons.
Side effects as well might be positive or negative, supplement-
ing an attainment of the initial objectives or supplanting it.
Thus the initial label of "boomerang" effect, while an apt description for this particular illustration, should not be retained
to categorize this type of phenomenon as a whole. Clearly
more work would be needed to tighten and strengthen these
suggestive categories.

While these reservations diminish the theoretical interest of
this model, Tocqueville's description highlights its important
psychological bearing. What his analysis uncovers in this case
is an important characteristic of individual and group decision making, the "cognitive rigidity" impeding a full rational
assessment of the crisis situation (Holsti, 1979; Kinder and
Weiss, 1978). To force old pictures into new frames is "to as-
similate incoming information to pre-existing images" (Jervis,
1976, 117). Surely the intention of the decision maker must be
to interpret the situation correctly and identify the best avail-

---

4 Tocqueville repeatedly criticized this dangerous reliance on political memory,
as Lively (1962, 30–31) documents at length.

able option, yet the analogical thinking naturally applied to this task often leads to different results.

Still Tocqueville's text reaches no clear verdict as to the irrationality of this "cognitive consistency" (Jervis, 1976, 119). Admittedly the decision to call on the National Guards might express a quest for "psychological harmony" with a predetermined definition of the situation, or manifest an organizational bias to rely on established standard operating procedures (in which case techniques of "crisis management" might remedy or cure the pathology of such a decision process). Yet the unhappy decision might also not be the result of any individual or institutional failure (and thus elude the therapeutic influence of any "crisis management" prescriptions). Focusing as he does on the unpredictable nature of the February Revolution, and examining the unanticipated "overshooting" mechanism that constituted its spring, Tocqueville might well conceive of this example of decision making in crisis as a limit case in which it would be rational, if sometimes unfortunate, to follow your most recent political experience. Considering the surprising pace of the events as well as their political significance, the accordingly "bounded rationality" (Simon, 1946) of the leaders could force the adoption of a less than optimal policy alternative. From this perspective the forcing of old pictures into new frames would be a nearly inevitable consequence of the sudden acceleration of the historical pace. The "cognitive closure" of the government in February 1848 could be seen as an unintended but predictable side effect of the "overshooting" phenomenon triggered by the opposition's revolutionary rhetoric.[5]

Chapter 5: "Undershooting"

Tocqueville's last example weaves together the previous theme of a misapplied political memory with the general

---

[5] Note that Elster (1978) as well includes decisions based on "correct technical rationality, but incorrect assumptions about initial conditions" under the category of "counterfinality."

mechanism of aggregation, a combination expressed in a metaphor Karl Marx later made famous, in reference to the very
same events: "The whole time I had the feeling that we had
staged a play about the French Revolution, rather than that we
were continuing it" (R, 53). The theater metaphor is exploited
to the limit: no "grandeur" in this spectacle, "no truth," but
a strange mix of "literary reminiscences" with "most serious demonstrations." Memories of real and imaginary revolutionary heroes rule people's minds, yet one senses no real
passion, no real fury, thus no real danger: "A tradition of
violent action was being followed, without real understanding, by frigid souls" (R, 53). Forever the detached aristocrat,
Tocqueville remarks: "Though I foresaw the terrible end to the
piece well enough, I could not take the actors very seriously;
the whole thing seemed a vile tragedy played by a provin-
cial troupe" (R, 53). Even while making a note to himself not
to overindulge in this happy metaphor (R, 74n4), Tocqueville
cannot resist coming back to it. A later passage mentions more
explicitly the literary sources (Thiers' *History of the Revolution* and Lamartine's *Girondins*) and theatrical productions
that rehabilitated the Terror and made it fashionable (R, 74).
The misplaced mimicking of past glories even carries over
to the Assembly, where once more factions distinguish themselves by topographical position, some to resume proudly the
title of Montagnards, and one deputy even obeys the ridiculous
decree of the Provisional Government to adopt "the dress of
the members of the Convention, in particular the white waist-
coat with turned-down collar always worn by actors playing
Robespierre" (R, 100; note the irony of Tocqueville's caustic
description).

However, the process of imitation does not exhaust the
analogy between the theater and the February Revolution; as
important is the result, or lack thereof—the political impotence of the revolutionary actors. Having started with a bang,
they ended in a whimper: their easy and complete triumph
(R, 72–73) bore no fruit. The revolutionaries utterly failed to

take advantage of their stunning victory (R, 96), to consolidate their control and reorganize the government and society. Again, though on the side of the popular opposition this time, political actors were "following examples from the past without understanding them" (R, 97) and thus without adapting to the new circumstances. For instance, notes Tocqueville, rather than establishing universal suffrage in the vain hope of summoning the people to support the revolution and promising the abolition of property rights (which a large share of the population was interested in preserving), they should have promised the abolition of debts (R, 97). Yet this case of a misguided recourse to historical patterns is complicated by the mere aggregation of political agents. The multiplication of heroes, brilliant demagogues, and visionary theorists (R, 74) necessarily spelled a dilution of quality and effectiveness; it also dissolved the revolutionary unity and disoriented the population, hence the "undershooting" effect of a victorious yet impotent revolution. One might think by analogy of the phenomenon of fashion (see R, 41, for a possible connection), in which a style loses its attractiveness and status appeal once it has successfully imposed itself throughout society. Just as diffusion lowers density, imitation lowers quality.

Intimations of this "undershooting" model can be found in *Democracy in America*. Noting that "unlike all physical forces, the power of thought is often actually increased by the small number of those expressing it," Tocqueville proceeded to deduce a social law from this premise: "It is an axiom of political science (there) that the only way to neutralize the effects of newspapers is to multiply their numbers. I cannot imagine why such a self-evident truth has not been more commonly accepted among us" (R, 181, 184).

Most striking in this instance of the February Revolution is the intimate connection between "overshooting" and "undershooting" effects. Both these disconcerting macrophenomena result from the spread of revolutionary sentiments through the larger population, leading to a sudden and powerful popular uprising but exhausting itself in the process. Tocqueville's account, by illuminating the unintended consequences produced through aggregation of microbehavior, uncovers the mechanism governing this initially puzzling political cycle.

Conclusion

This sketch of one possible reading of the first part of the *Recollections* is predicated on a conception of Tocqueville as a social scientist, and not only a historian and political commentator. These labels are meant to stand for a combination of theoretical goals: care and talent for ideographic study do not necessarily spell a lack of interest or achievement in stating nomological conclusions. Indeed, Tocqueville attempted to stake a position between two extremes of exclusive concern for either the particular or the general, either the historically or the analytically true. To vindicate this description of Tocqueville's approach, and thus strengthen the reading, will be the task of this conclusion.

However implicit their presentation, three formal models of behavior clearly informed Tocqueville's analyses. His discursive style does not prevent their relatively easy detection and their subsequent reformulation in more abstract terms. In translation to contemporary jargon one could summarize Tocqueville's offerings in these five chapters as two models of microbehavior explaining contradictory macrophenomena of rapid change—"overshooting" and "undershooting"—and one model of decision making under uncertainty: "cognitive closure" resulting from a reliance on dated information in crisis situations. All three models offer abstract, general explanations of unintended consequences of political action. All three are anchored in methodological individualism and assume rational, self-interested actors. Yet uneasiness with such theoretical reformulations persists: more than a mere lack of technical jargon lay behind Tocqueville's reluctance to explicitly offer such analytical, formal models.

Immediately following his five-chapter study in the unintended consequences of political action, Tocqueville situates his thought using a contrast between "literary men" on the one hand and "politicians" on the other (R, 61–62). Reference to this split between two provinces of the political world, the theoretical and the practical, is made in *The Old Regime and the French Revolution* (1955, pt. III, ch. 1) which was written around the same time. In setting this dichotomy Tocqueville harks back to a distinction introduced at the outset (R, 17) and used throughout his analysis. The two ideal types, drawn from his personal experience, characterize two extreme approaches to reflection on politics, the first focusing on "general causes" and the second on "accidents." Theorists, for such are Tocqueville's "literary men," "see general causes everywhere," and boast of broad generalizations of "mathematical exactness" (R, 62). Tocqueville's reaction to such claims suffers from no ambivalence: "For my part I hate all those absolute systems that make all the events of history depend on great first causes linked together by the chain of fate and thus succeed, so to speak, in banishing men from the history of the human race" (R, 62). Yet politicians' interpretations are not granted a warmer welcome. Their obsession with the particular, with the petty incidents demanding the greatest share of their professional attention, disqualifies their judgment as well: "Spending their lives amid the disconnected events of each day, [they] freely attribute everything to particular incidents and think that all the little strings their hands are busy pulling daily are those that control the world's fate" (R, 62).

In truth, these opposed ideal types draw on a distinction already elaborated in *Democracy in America* (1969, vol. 2, pt. I, ch. 20). There the reference is to a split between two provinces of the theoretical world, between democratic and aristocratic historians. The first naturally view history from an abstract, leveling perspective, while the second indulge in a fascination for outstanding individual actions. The same sociology of knowledge applies here: politicians as a rule—being a small aristocracy of political actors—seem to suffer from a professional disease limiting their sights to the specific and particular. Clearly, in Tocqueville's opinion, both nomologists and ideographs—both exclusive emphases on universal causes or particular accidents—are wrong. Indeed in one respect they share the same error, which Tocqueville, in locating himself between these two extremes,[6] points out. Some historical facts necessarily remain inexplicable—a conclusion neither brand of theorist would remain satisfied with—while others can be explained only by accidental circumstances. Elaborating on this conception, which frustrates both determinist philosophies of history and individualistic beliefs in historical intentionality, Tocqueville introduces a notion of "chance" well worth examining: "Chance, or rather the concatenation of secondary causes, which we call by that name because we can't sort them all out, is a very important element in all that we see taking place in the world's theatre" (R, 62).

Surely the attempt of the first five chapters was to pursue patiently the ramifications of secondary causes, the aggregation of individual reactions leading to seemingly random, chance events. Tocqueville in fact faithfully followed his method as defined in this passage, a combination of the broad nomological vision with the ideographic attention to details, sorting out "chance" amid the general circumstances without which it can do nothing (R, 62). Indeed the very first chapter set this crucial background, presenting one by one the "antecedent facts, the nature of institutions, turns of mind and the state of mores [which] are the material from which chance composes those impromptu events that surprise and terrify us" (R, 62). In tracking down the unintended consequences of political action against this sociocultural background, Tocqueville refused to

---

[6] For further evidence of this location, see Tocqueville's letter to Louis de Kergolay, dated December 15, 1850, the period during which the *Recollections* were written (SL, 253).

dictate general laws of historical development covering the universal yet he uncovered abstract models applicable toward the intelligibility of the particular.[7] However obvious these might seem in retrospect, they coherently organize the seeming chaos of February 1848, and cogently explain its surprising pace.[8]

[7] Richter notes Tocqueville's concept of "chance" as a concatenation of events, yet finds it unclear, because chance for Tocqueville does nothing unprepared; Richter (1966, 115–16) blames Tocqueville for being insufficiently technical and overly unphilosophical.

[8] For a comprehensive survey of contemporary reactions to and modern judgment of this revolution ("by no means an inevitable revolution," "an effect out of proportion to its cause"), see Zeldin (1973, 468–69).

CHAPTER 3

Formal Models, in Tocqueville and in Social Theory

The argument of the preceding case study now must be generalized, on two ascending levels: Are formal models a recurrent, intrinsic element of Tocqueville's method? Do their potential contributions and possible detractions, on balance, justify viewing them as an essential component of social theory? By answering both queries affirmatively my argument challenges most conventional canons of scholarship. First, Tocqueville is commonly regarded as a discursive, even literary forerunner of social science: the traditional answer to the first question above remains negative. Second, most proponents of one of the two major strands in contemporary social theory—the hermeneutic, "continental" school (a misleading but now convenient appellation)—customarily reject formal modeling as a misguided and dangerous positivist intrusion into the human sciences. Their resolute answer to the second question above would be negative as well. (In contrast, at least a number of the advocates of formal modeling would resent the qualification of their approach as merely a component of social theory.) Finally, most scientifically inclined theorists are likely to hold the conventional image of Tocqueville, while precisely the classically, hermeneutically inclined ones have been prone to detect in his work a (regrettable in their eyes) tendency for formal, abstract generalizations.[1] Thus a positive answer to the first question most probably would be accompanied by a negative one to the second, and vice versa, the intersection of two positive answers remaining mostly empty.[2] To establish convincingly the validity of such a combination calls for a preliminary elucidation of the notion of "formal models" itself.

Formal Models Generally

For simplicity's sake, beginning somewhat illogically with a consideration of the secondary characterization "formal" might be forgiven. Ostensibly the qualifier "formal" refers to the symbolic medium in which the analysis is carried out. Translation into a less informal, more carefully defined language aims at avoiding the ambiguities and complexities of ordinary language to achieve greater precision. Insofar as this ambition derives from a belief in the possibility of devising a purely neutral language, free from any sociologically or subjectively induced normative components, it remains delusory: at a minimum the reference from and back to a given perception of the empirical world necessarily hinges on such components. More naive and unfounded still would be a faith in mathematics (or any other formal language) as a privileged access to ultimate reality. However comforting metaphysically, a correspondence between any such artifacts and ontology appears entirely circular logically, reality being constituted by our application of our concepts. Yet as long as the argu-

---

[1] Pierson (1959) and, following him, Bradley (1945) and Richter (1970) illustrate the latter tendency. Clearly the earlier, complementary one does not lend itself to easy demonstration: a claimed absence is hard to document, and easy to disprove. Note though that even social scientists who do discuss Tocqueville's achievements as a scientific theorist tend to put him down: Stinchcombe (1978) compares him unfavorably to Trostky, and Smelser (1971) criticizes his lack of scientific rigor.

[2] Boudon (1981, 1982) remains to my knowledge the sole exception. Commentators inclined toward two negative answers are easier to find: Salomon (1935, 1939, 1959) and Zetterbaum (1967, 1972) offer two fitting examples.

ment for formalization turns on the commitment to achieve a greater degree of definiteness and, for some tasks at least, of flexibility, its validity seems unchallengeable. While consistency, precision, and ultimately logical validity are properties of the argument itself, such careful reasoning might be easier in some languages than others. The intrinsic structure of formal languages demands a high degree of precision and explicitness, and facilitates the presentation of lengthy chains of implications (for a similar argument, see Kramer and Hertzberg, 1975, 353).[3]

A more sanguine defense of formalization, which indeed would imply a rejection of my reference to this process of translation as a secondary characteristic, has been given by Herbert Simon. Simon objects in principle to a merely quantitative advocacy of formalization as a matter of ascending degrees of precision. Rather, he claims, formal languages are qualitatively superior: mathematical translation in itself constitutes a substantive contribution to theory, because "it permits clear and rigorous reasoning about phenomena too complex to be handled in words" (1957, 89). This advantage of formalization over cruder languages "should prove of even greater significance in the social sciences, which deal with phenomena of the greatest complexity, than it has in the natural sciences" (Simon, 1957, 89).

Several lines of counterargument to this claim can be developed. Conceivably, the degree of complexity possible through the manipulation of formal language might exceed our ability to translate the results back into practice. Mathematical operations on symbols might lack recognizable equivalents in the informal language through which we understand and act upon our world. A formal language too superior in its complexity to our informal discourse might produce an abundance of

---

[3] I am charitably omitting Kramer and Hertzberg's example, a comparison between English (the language, say, of Talcott Parsons) and French (the language, say, of Descartes) as an illustration of descending degrees of precision in language (1975, 353).

remarkably sophisticated results, devoid of any significance. This seemingly paradoxical conclusion has been stated by L. A. Zadeh (1973, 28) as the "principle of incompatibility," whereby beyond a certain threshold of complexity in the system studied precision and significance become almost mutually exclusive characteristics.

Conversely, one might argue that precisely the rigid precision of formal languages fails to capture the complexity of social reality. Computer scientists, for example, have long recognized the skill with which human beings understand and operate on the vague concepts of informal discourse. By contrast the rigorous processing of strictly defined concepts limits the computer's ability to duplicate fundamental conceptual functions. Consequently a partial return to linguistic variables as qualifiers of numeric functions—a combination known as "fuzzy logic"—has been advocated (Santos, 1970; Zadeh, 1973). Vagueness, it would seem, has its advantages, certainly in "describing and explaining how people interact with the world around them" (Hersh and Caramazza, 1976).

These two contrasting yet complementary qualifications of the claims made on behalf of formalization justify a cautious, pragmatic approach to the translation into formal language. An ad hoc balancing of the possibly contradictory demands for precision, relevance, and flexibility should determine the amount and degree of formalization desirable in each case. More vindictive arguments against formalization, however, seem unjustified. Undoubtedly any retreat from ordinary language must result in a further estrangement from the wider public: this seems to be the bane of all scientific discourse. While the "human sciences" should be especially concerned about the connection with the lay audience, even those of their practitioners who prefer this appellation and acknowledge this duty have failed to refrain from esoteric jargons (see, for a striking example, Adorno's demonstrations against Heidegger's obscure language, 1973a, and his defense of his own, 1973b, 18–19). At issue is not the reliance on a specialized terminology, but rather the commitment to return to informal discourse with one's arguments and conclusions. Finally, the suspicion that formal manipulations of symbols all too easily conceal instrumental manipulations of human beings seems unwarranted. The connection between formalization and objectification is spurious, as the moral and political attitudes of the theorist can find their expression equally well in formal and informal garb (witness the reification of metaphysical categories and objectification of persons in numerous traditional philosophic discourses).

Having found formalization to be a variable, secondary characteristic, it is time to examine the substantive element in formal models, the process of modeling. As a theoretical strategy to address the complexity of human affairs, modeling entails a selection of interactions deemed essential, and a recreation of their abstract structure. In practice, then, a model operates on two levels: it offers a homeomorph (identical in structure) of the microsocial episode, and presents a paramorph of the processes of its production (Harré, 1976, 30–31). Evidently the key mechanism of modeling consists of an empowering simplification, whose simultaneous counterpart is an impoverishing reductionism: as assumptions accumulate, conclusions gain in general applicability what they lose in specific relevance. This approach clearly fits the aspirations of a social science intent on emulating the achievements of natural science—the attainment of universal, covering laws of human interaction. Thus Barry (1978, 4–5) considers modeling the initial, identifying step in the "economic approach": deliberately simplifying the phenomenon studied, positing a number of actors, and deducing their interaction given certain assumptions about the rationality of their behavior. This particular method of "vicarious problem solving" (Schelling, 1978, 18) has profoundly altered the social sciences through the development of game theory and public choice theory. It now represents the most successful expression of Hume's age-old ambition "that politics may be reduced to a science"

(1952). Hume's formulation at least had the saving grace of openly admitting the reductionist character of the endeavor, while some modern-day followers mistakenly conflate abstract simplification and interdisciplinarity (see for example Becker, 1976, ch. 1; Hamburger, 1979, 8). Postponing momentarily a discussion of these ambitions, and by extension of the advantages and disadvantages of the approach as a whole, I now turn to the first question raised at the outset: Were formal models a recurrent, intrinsic element of Tocqueville's method?

Formal Models in Tocqueville

One observation can be made even before engaging specific texts. Tocqueville did not rely on formal languages of any kind, either in the presentation of his final arguments or, insofar as we can surmise from his notebooks, in the process of their development. Given the relatively accessory role of formalization, however, this realization does not prejudge the question of his reliance on the approach generally: discursive presentations can still elaborate highly abstract models and equally broad conclusions. In fact, recent surveys of social theory admit the persistent rarity and simplicity of formalization in the field (Moulin, 1982, 3), noting that formal theory in political science, for example, would be considered the ordinary, garden variety of scientific theory as a whole (Kramer and Hertzberg, 1975, 352). Thus the absence of formalization in the writings of a mid-nineteenth century, best-selling author such as Tocqueville cannot be taken as an indication of his ignorance or rejection of abstract modeling as a theoretical strategy. Such a conclusion would confuse *opus operatum* and *modus operandi*—the finished product with the process of production. Rather, much could be learned from Tocqueville's masterful use of ordinary discourse in developing and presenting general conclusions.

Similarly, the absence of explicit references to modeling, especially given the late blooming of such social scientific methodological terminology and methodological discourse generally, carries no great weight. For the purposes of this argument, Tocqueville might well be the Monsieur Jourdain of modeling: it would be perfectly satisfactory if a case could be made that Tocqueville's attempts to explain complex social interactions in effect revolved around models of the type game theory and social choice theory develop in more formal fashion. At stake is the presence and importance of such reasoning in Tocqueville's approach. Finally, as a last note of caution on this issue, Tocqueville's refusal to fully develop abstract models generating universal laws might well constitute at least an implicit expression of his reticence to wholly endorse the program of a science of society. To confirm this possibility a closer look at his work is needed.

Chronologically the closest of Tocqueville's great works to the *Recollections, The Old Regime and the French Revolution* offers a wealth of informal yet well-developed models. Tocqueville's demographic analysis of workers' migration in eighteenth-century France (pt. II, ch. 7) constitutes a simple example of this approach: a straightforward, homo economicus rationality is assumed to motivate these migrant workers, and the industrial tax structure provides a clear matrix of payoffs. Accordingly in the sixty years preceding the revolution, Louis XVI's policy actually provoked at least a doubling of the number of workers in Paris and encouraged their concentration in certain districts (notably the Faubourg St.-Antoine) (AR, 75–76). More subtle deductions still result from other applications of this approach. Though the economic situation of the bourgeoisie and aristocracy were leveling off—one improving as the other deteriorated—no stable coalition was created, a rift that proved fatal to the stability of the regime (AR, pt. II, ch. 10). A special tax, the *droits de franc-fief*, had been leveled on commoners owning lands properly accruing to the nobility. Thus no common cause on this all-important form of property ownership was allowed to develop, thereby exacerbating the class struggle in eighteenth-century France (AR, 102–3; see also AR, 88).

In both analyses Tocqueville explores the relation between the characteristic behavior of individuals belonging to a given economic class and the characteristics of the aggregate, the sociopolitical situation. His mode of analysis is retrospective, attempting to figure out intentions and models of behavior that could have led to the historical pattern observed (for these methodological distinctions, see Schelling, 1978, 13). Throughout, however, Tocqueville's viewpoint remains that of the ruler, the politician who through legislation controls the rules of the game, altering the payoffs for all participants (see Hamburger, 1979, 4).

While the examples adduced so far are confined to the analysis of specific social episodes, Tocqueville was willing at times to deduce generally applicable laws. His examination of the dynamics of interest groups led him to a conclusion familiar from the recent "public goods" literature. The free-rider problem increases as the size of the group increases. In small associations, Tocqueville observes, the utmost concern was shown for the group's interests: "For its members were acutely aware that they had to defend their group privileges and prestige; no individual could play for safety and make ignoble concessions, hoping to pass unnoticed. The stage on which each played his part was small but brightly lit and there was always the same audience to applaud or hiss him" (AR, 115). There is no need to downplay the merits of Olson's celebrated analysis (1965), especially given its more cautious examination of other influential factors in this dynamic (various "selective incentives," "latency" of interest groups, "exclusivity" and "inclusivity"). Yet, however discursively and indeed matter-of-factly presented, the fundamental logic of collective action is captured in Tocqueville's analysis and rendered comprehensible to the lay reader.

Tocqueville's application of this rational choice modeling

approach led on occasion to results of great subtlety and complexity. Thus, an astute selection of key strategic interactions
explained at once the rapid spread of urbanization and the
slow growth of a capitalist agriculture in France as opposed to
England. Boudon, the sole commentator to notice and elaborate on Tocqueville's extensive use of models, chose these related analyses as his main example (1981, 32–33, 60–61). Even
today a quick glance at a map will confirm the surprising
number of small towns in France, while a look at eighteenth-
century statistics will evidence the peculiarly slow development of agriculture and commerce there. Both macrosociological effects, according to Tocqueville, can be traced back to
the rationally motivated behavior of individuals in light of the
existing social structure. Administrative centralization under
the Old Regime generated a growing, nearly elastic supply
of offices, which entailed economic as well as status-related
advantages (tax reductions and possible ennoblement). Land-
owners, particularly small holders, therefore chose to leave
their land more often on the average than in England, hence
the comparative underdevelopment of agriculture and multiplication of small towns (AR, 90–91; 123–24). Clearly, in
this case, the resulting developments were not consciously
planned by the individual actors or the legislating authority.
Rather, these macrosociological phenomena once more illustrate the mechanism of unintentional consequences of individual actions. Boudon developed this point as well (1982,
105–7).

Unquestionably the greatest theoretical contribution of *The
Old Regime and the French Revolution* remains "Tocqueville's
paradox" (Boudon, 1982, 4): the discovery of the dialectical
relation between material plenty and individual satisfaction.
Tocqueville's demonstration that a rapid increase in general
welfare hastened the outbreak of the French Revolution stands
at the center of his interpretation (AR, pt. III, ch. 4). Its import
is to characterize the revolution as an unintended consequence
of naively benevolent policies (AR, pt. III, ch. 5). Tocqueville's

insight, articulated further through the notions of "relative deprivation" and "frame of reference" (Runciman, 1966), has generated at least a couple of well-known formalizations: the concept of "the phenomenon of rising expectations" and the model of the "J curve." Yet, despite this legacy, it might be argued that, however fruitful the initial insight, Tocqueville himself never developed the logic of relative frustration. An examination of Tocqueville's other major work, *Democracy in America*, will dispel this claim.

At least three different analyses in *Democracy in America* revolve around the logic of relative frustration: Tocqueville's examination of the restlessness of Americans (vol. 2, pt. II, ch. 13), his explanation of the comparative scarcity of lofty ambitions in the United States (vol. 2, pt. III, ch. 19), and his grim foreshadowing of the dangers of place hunting for democracy (vol. 2, pt. III, ch. 20). Translated into modern sociological jargon, Tocqueville's language loses much of its accessibility and rhetorical power; in particular, the three succinct paragraphs describing the effects of equality on restlessness and frustration deserve rereading, as a brilliant instance of Tocqueville's lucid style (DA, 537). Tocqueville's important insights, however, lose nothing in the process. In the absence of social stratification, an equalization of opportunities initially will induce illusions of rapid advancement in many, leading to a growth in frustration: unfortunately, the inelasticity in the number of great positions and careers clashes with the sudden expansion in the number of ambitious fortune-seekers (DA, 537). Such is the law of competition (DA, 630). Moreover, when this effect becomes clear, the participants readjust their hopes and limit their vision (DA, 631), a result reinforced by the desire of the democratic regime to regulate advancement according to strict equality by submitting all candidates to a multitude of equal tests (DA, 630). A further, ultimate consequence, which Tocqueville plainly delineates with regard to European (and especially French) practices, is that any attempt by a centralized administration to provide sufficient alterna-

tive roads for ambition are bound to fail. Such long-range incapacity to satisfy the growing demand of a mistakenly enticed
public will endanger the very existence of any state pursuing
this policy (DA, 634).

Tocqueville's analyses can be elaborated further, along
narrower psychological or broad sociological lines. Samuel
Stouffer's application of reference-group theory to explain the
rise in dissatisfaction among military units where the chances
of promotion were higher remains the classic example of
the microsociological approach (Stouffer et al., 1965); Émile
Durkheim's interpretation of different types of suicides adum-
brated a theory of the macrosociological kind (1951, see e.g.
285–87). Undeniably Tocqueville's own explanations hinged
on both approaches. Yet it has been shown that a formal
model of the structure of opportunities and probabilities of rewards captures the underlying logic of both types of reasoning
(Boudon, 1981, 79–80; see also 1982, ch. 5). A favorable alter-
ation of the range of opportunities, without a proportional
modification of the availability of rewards, can magnify the
number of individuals opting to try their luck, and thus diminish the probability of rewards. This basic model lies behind
Tocqueville's initial analysis (DA, 537).

Other examples of Tocqueville's reliance on abstract models,
of which there are many in such a massive work as *Democracy in America*, exhibit his facility with schematic "game-
theoretic" reasoning. The section on "Public Expenses" in the
chapter on "Government by Democracy in America" (DA,
vol. 1, pt. II, ch. 5) presents a highly simplified theoretical
model to illuminate the relations between tax legislation and
class structure. Assuming three broad economic classes, and a
simple alternation of legislative authority among them, three
possible taxation schemes can be deduced: in each hypothetical case, the typical interest of an average member of the class
in control will dictate the proportion of the tax burden. One
could quarrel with Tocqueville's specific assumptions (for example his possible underestimation of greed among the very

rich); yet not only does his conclusion remain plausible—middle-class rule would be the most economical on public expenditures—but his reasoning clearly proceeds on the basis of abstract modeling, and his conclusions are cast in the form of general laws. These methodological aspects alone matter for this examination.

Similarly, one of Tocqueville's arguments for augmenting the number of juries comes as close as ordinary language can to mathematical deduction: given a fixed rate of mortality a great number of judicial positions contributes to a greater mobility and thus a continual excitement of ambition, which makes judges dangerously susceptible to public opinion and private influences. A greater reliance on juries could eliminate this problem (as well as a related one, the increasing probability of incompetence in proportion to the number of judges) (DA, 272n4). Yet another abstract demonstration illustrates the collective suboptimality of individual rationality. Entrepreneurs all collectively agree on the undesirability of state intervention in the economy, yet they do not hesitate to call on its help for their own special (and urgent) needs; thus "the passions of individuals, in spite of themselves, promote" the growth of centralized power (DA, 672).

As this last deduction underscores, Tocqueville's reasoning derives from a primary assumption as to the self-interested motivation of all actors. The point was made earlier in relation to the models in *The Old Regime and the French Revolution*; *Democracy in America*, however, offers an explicit elaboration of this model of man. The encounter with American democracy forced Tocqueville to refine his conception: not only were aristocratic heroism, saintly self-abnegation, and patriotic sacrifice not to be expected anymore, but egotism, if only enlightened, could be relied on instead to some extent. This theme was first sounded in the introduction (DA, 15–16), and Tocqueville emphasized the crucial role of self-interest as a prime moving force throughout the analyses of the first volume (e.g. DA, 175; DA, 239). However, Tocqueville's most developed discussions of "the doctrine of self-interest properly understood" were reserved for chapters 8 and 9 in the second part of the second volume. His examination there makes it clear that the maintenance of public order and civic virtue requires more than a straightforward selfishness. What he figuratively describes in one place as the mixture in man of angel and brute (DA, 546), he literally specifies in these pages as the learning of gratification-delay (DA, 529). This restraint, which in contemporary formal jargon would be termed an extension of the time-horizon, can be acquired only through education (DA, 528–29). Its beneficial effects were always implicitly recognized (DA, 525), especially by religious leaders (DA, 529), who perceived that the thought of death and the afterworld could serve to encourage virtues in this world. Indeed Tocqueville paraphrases Pascal's wager—a pure game-theoretic model—to underscore the self-interested calculation behind at least the vulgar kind of popular religion. This model of man, with its implicit transition from ancient virtue to modern self-interested prudence, informed the methodological individualism of Tocqueville's formal models and encouraged the reliance on the approach as a whole.[4]

Other instances of Tocqueville's application of modeling certainly could be reported. However, those examined here should suffice to demonstrate the extent of his reliance on the methodology and to illustrate its wide range. When reaching for an explanation of phenomena involving complex social interactions, Tocqueville repeatedly devised an abstract model detailing the appropriate rational behaviors of the actors involved and deducing the results, often unintended, of their combination. Some of his most penetrating insights and most far-reaching generalizations derived from this type of reason-

---

[4] See Schleifer (1980, 235) for additional support from Tocqueville's notes and letters concerning the replacement of virtue by the "social theory" of self-interest (in particular the letter to Chabrol). Jardin's analysis of Tocqueville's research methods in the study of the French Revolution further illustrates Tocqueville's methodological individualism (1984, 461).

ing. Boudon's conclusion that Tocqueville's analyses "always have an analogous structure (1979, 57), meaning they rely on quasi-formal models describing abstract systems of interaction, is upheld by this review—insofar as the analyses of complex interactions are involved. Yet the initial question regarding Tocqueville's possible reticence to endorse completely the program of a science of society, in particular as it bears on the only semiformal representation of his models, still awaits an answer. Was Mill entitled to conclude that Tocqueville's approach was "the true Baconian and Newtonian method applied to society" (1961, viii)? Addressing this question forces a detour through another, prior one. What are the advantages and disadvantages of this scientific approach generally? Clarifying both the place of causality and the danger of determinism in social science will make Tocqueville's attitude toward it more easily intelligible.

The Place of Causality

In line with earlier strictures against "high methodology," the ontological groundings of the scientific approach to society will be disregarded. It would be too easy, for example, to deride the circularity of Mill's own derivation of the four methods of experimental inquiry. Their elaboration relies on the existence of regular and recurrent sequential relations—"laws of nature"—which we validate through the application of the methodology (Hindess, 1977, 197). From a more pragmatic perspective, the most significant characteristic of the scientific approach remains the elimination of the category of "purpose" (Bauman, 1978, 11): causality replaces teleology and intentionality.[5] Tocqueville's contemporary, Auguste Comte, hailed this shift as a cleaning of all metaphysical and theological vestiges in favor of a truly "positive" approach. Without neces-

---

[5] Functionalism, in biology for example (but see applications to social science, e.g. Cohen, 1978), presents an odd mixture of both vocabularies; the continuing debate on its validity as an explanatory scheme in social theory need not be addressed here (see Elster, 1983a; Van Parijs, 1981).

sarily subscribing either to his interpretation or to his ultimate goal, we must recognize the crucial import of the category of causality in explaining human behavior. From the hypotheses of sociobiology to the analyses of macrosociological interaction, causal explanations have illuminated a plethora of previously enigmatic phenomena. Even the best proponents of the rival, hermeneutic approach to social theory acknowledge this fruitful contribution. Against Winch's "hermeneutical social theory," Giddens argues for the importance of causal laws in social science (1984, 221, 229); against Rickert's exclusive *verstehen* psychology, Betti argues for a general, structural approach (Bleicher, 1980, 44). Significantly, both criticisms emphasize the same range of phenomena, above and below the reach of intentionality: the unconscious motivations and the unintended consequences of action.

Both types of phenomena elude the control of the agent—under normal circumstances, we do not know the unconscious sources of our behavior, nor do we anticipate its unintended effects. This realization at once limits the scope of intentional interpretation and opens a wide field for causal explanation (Giddens, 1984, 224; Elster, 1983a, 20). Establishing psychological social laws, however, poses a special challenge: at least given the present state of scientific knowledge, we cannot independently identify mental states, a prerequisite for verifying any causal link (MacIntyre, 1973, 20). Thus causal connections between motivations and actions are not currently possible (Davidson, 1980, 232; note that Davidson argues against the possibility of such psychophysical laws *in principle*). As a result the macrosociological study of unintended consequences has been more attractive to social theorists and can claim greater achievements.

The tradition of concern for unintended consequences is well established. Ferguson's original mention of "the result of human action, but not the execution of any human design" (1767, 187) probably informed Mandeville's better known satiric "Fable of the Bees" (1924), in which the initial poem concluded that

The worst of all the multitudes
Did something for the common good.

From here the road to Adam Smith's "invisible hand" was short. A more philosophical generalization can be found in Hegel's "cunning of reason" as well as his dialectical logic of "contradictions," translated into the language of politics by Marx, who somewhat cryptically commented that "men make their own history, but they do not make it just as they please" (in Tucker, 1978, 595). On these premises Sartre (1976, 232ff) discussed the curse of "counterfinality" haunting human action, while Arendt (1958, 190)—nearly alone among contemporary political theorists—reflected on the unexpected results of political action reverberating among human plurality.

Unsurprisingly, the realization that such a formidable battery of thinkers shares a similar concern with unintended consequences prompted a number of strong reactions. Following Carl Menger's reminder, at the close of the previous century (1883, 182), Friedrich von Hayek and later Karl Popper both defined "the main task of the theoretical social science" to be the tracing of the "unintended social repercussions of intentional human action" (Popper, 1963, 342; Hayek, 1967, 97). This prescription was echoed by Ernest Nagel as well (1952, 54). Robert Merton's seminal article, "The Unanticipated Consequences of Purposive Social Action" (1936), together with his subsequent work on self-altering prophecies (1948)—which generated a great deal of theoretical reflection (Buck, 1963; Henshel and Kennedy, 1973; Vetterling, 1976; Henshel, 1982)—were responsible for much of this resurgence of interest.

Nevertheless, despite these numerous efforts, the remark of Raymond Boudon, perhaps the foremost social theorist in the field of unintended consequences, that even a summary classification of these effects has scarcely been attempted (1981, xvii), remains true to this day. Political studies appear still more barren in this respect; adding Tocqueville to the list of great theorists preoccupied with this issue might encour-

age some fresh reflection on the unintended consequences of
political action. As the previous case study as well as the examination in this chapter demonstrated, Tocqueville's use of
formal models was directed principally toward the elucidation of such effects. Concatenations of individual actions were
shown to cause, given a specific structure of interaction, certain macrosociological phenomena. The insights generated by
these analyses, and generally the magnitude and importance
of the field open to causal explanation in social theory as
a whole, need no further elaboration. Rather the limits to
subsumption under abstract, universal causal laws should be
stressed.

The Danger of Determinism

In their eagerness to emulate a conception of "hard science," itself under attack recently (Bernstein, 1983, 20–24),
social scientists might forget the essential interpretive residual of their causal explanations.[6] Though stressed once before,
the point deserves reiteration: insofar as causes for action are
implicated, the necessary passage through mental states re-
introduces a purely interpretive moment in the explanation.[7]
Insistence on this caveat is justified not merely for considerations of logical precision, but rather for its broad moral and
political significance: a complete causal theory of human behavior would entail determinism. By itself, the effort of social
theory to convert the contingent into the necessary carries conservative overtones, in making reality appear more entrenched
than before (Hirschman, 1971, 354).[8] When joined by a will

[6] Consider the following dangerous lapse of a particularly careful social theorist: "First, all phenomena covered by intentional explanation can also be explained causally. . . . Of course, to say that the agent's doing p was caused by the
desire to do p, is not to give a causal explanation. It is only to rephrase the intentional explanation in such a way as to indicate the existence of some (unknown)
causal explanation. Nevertheless I shall have occasion to use this language of
beliefs and desires causing action, as it is very convenient for many purposes"
(Elster, 1983a, 19–20, 22).

[7] I develop this point further in my "What Are Preference Explanations?"
Hadari, 1987.

[8] Note that "overtones" do not have the status of logical implications: in some

to subsume all subject matter under causal categories, it eliminates responsibility, sucking the life blood from our moral notions (Berlin, 1969). Tocqueville's virulent attack against "absolute systems" that ban men from history (see above, p. 27)
stemmed from a realization of these dangerous implications.
Its modern echo, complete with a reformulation of the two
extreme theoretical attitudes Tocqueville denigrated (abstract,
causal, and deterministic versus particular, interpretive, and
contingent), can be found in Sir Isaiah Berlin's work (see, for
example, 1969, xxvi; 1978, ch. 1, "The Hedgehog and the
Fox"). Both these liberal pluralists recoil before the fatalist
overtones of the program of a science of society. No better
expression of Tocqueville's (1908) sentiments can be found
than his celebrated correspondence with Gobineau.

The gist of the dispute between Tocqueville and his younger
protégé, provoked by the latter's publication of the infamous
Essai sur l'inégalité de races humaines, was philosophical determinism. Tocqueville rightly detected in Gobineau's racist
hypotheses, despite the author's protest, a materialist theory
of predestination. Intellectually, he believed it probably false;
in terms of practical consequences, however, he deemed it
most certainly pernicious. Any deduction of inflexible causal
forces ruling human behavior, Tocqueville explained, implies a
great restriction, if not the complete abolition, of human freedom. Rather than developing an abstract and general social
science at this price, social theorists should retain the traditional respect for individuality and particularity.[9] In truth, a
deeper analysis of the relation between "objective determinism" and "subjective freedom" would belie the inevitability
of such a trade-off between them (Bourdieu, 1984, 44). Mastery of causal determinations need not translate into predic-
tive knowledge, hence need not deny the freedom of histori-

---

cases uncovering necessity makes better control hence more extensive choice possible. (See Bourdieu, 1984, 44–45.)

[9] John Stone and Stephen Mennell offer a translation of a representative extract from this correspondence (1980, 320–22); see also SL, 297–301. I believe
Nef's reading (1963) to be biased toward a consideration of the religious—and
specifically Christian—aspect of the dispute.

cal agents (MacIntyre, 1984, 100). Indeed the permanence of
sources of radical unpredictability in social life—examined at
the end of this section—maintains this conceptual asymme-
try between explanation and prediction, and thus preserves
the rewards and burdens of free will (Boudon, 1985, 166).
Tocqueville, though, while aware of the beneficial impenetra-
bility of "chance," labored to secure an even higher degree of
individual opacity and historical unpredictability.

His whole theoretical practice was undertaken in this spirit.
No ultimate determination of any social aspect by another—
as in Marx's crudest distinctions between superstructure and
infrastructure—and no reduction to other realms—as in Lévi-
Strauss's occasional digressions on the supremacy of chemistry
—were admitted. Tocqueville remained, throughout, a proba-
bilist (Aron, 1964, 166), never a prophet. Indeed a main lesson
of the *Recollections*, as the case study emphasized, was to
stress the limitations on prospective political judgment. Once
more, an intellectual and practical reason for this caution can
be discerned. The latter should be obvious: in Tocqueville's
conception of the task of social theory, a special place was
reserved for a defense of diversity and creativity, for a cultivation of respect for the unique and spontaneous (Hirschman's
"possibilism" partakes of this spirit, 1971, 27). Here at last
an answer to our earlier query emerges: not merely a lack of
intellectual rigor prevented Tocqueville from presenting more
than "nascent" theoretical models (Smelser, 1971, 44). Style in
this case followed substance. The discursive formulation of his
models underscored the embeddedness of general explanatory
schemes in particular contexts, and highlighted Tocqueville's
reluctance to proffer universal, ahistorical laws of behavior.
Such an attitude ruled out any peremptory proclamation of
definite prophecies.

One may adduce, however, a more theoretical reason for
eschewing overdetermined predictions in social science. While
retrospective analysis can often demonstrate the necessity of
an earlier social configuration for the emergence of a later

one, the seemingly symmetrical opposite conceptual operation proves much more difficult. Given the staggering multiplicity of intervening factors—in contrast to the abstract reductionism of formal models—the social theorist usually can do no more than anticipate a range of possible developments (Elias, 1978, 160–61). However astute our deduction of complex interactions, some elements will elude our grasp. Tocqueville's notion of "chance," introduced at the end of the previous chapter, is meant to underscore this irreducible unpredictability: "It is difficult enough for the human mind to trace some sort of great circle around the future, but within that circle chance plays a part that can never be grasped. In any vision of the future, chance always forms a blind spot which the mind's eye can never penetrate" (DA, 357). Thus, for instance, even Tocqueville's unforgiving sociology of knowledge carefully allowed for individual exceptions (e.g. DA, 474). Accordingly his celebrated "prophecy" as to the "fated progress of equality" must be understood as a (well-based) historical conjecture, indeed stated in a manner underlining its vagueness, and proclaimed in the hope mankind would seize the opportunity to direct its course (DA, 12).[10]

A more systematic examination can be offered to shore up Tocqueville's notion of "chance." At least three sources of radical unpredictability in social life appear permanent. Absolute innovation, often under the guise of a specific—hence unforeseeable—solution to a diffuse problem, is tautologically unpredictable (MacIntyre, 1984, 94; Boudon, 1985, 177–79). Pure contingency (MacIntyre, 1984, 99–100), the fortuitous encounter between two independent causal chains scientifi-

---

[10] Tocqueville might have succumbed, at times, to the temptation of posing as a prophet; for those small sins, however, he was repentant: "I humbly confess (as it might in effect appear humiliating for a man who sometimes meddled in prophecy) that I see absolutely nothing in the night in which we are. I understand neither how this could last nor how it could end. I see myself without a compass, without a rudder and without oars on a sea whose coast I nowhere perceive, and, tired from my vain agitation, I crouch at the bottom of the boat and await the future" (Tocqueville to Mme. de Circourt, June 6, 1850; OC, XVIII, 34).

cally termed a Cournot effect (Boudon, 1984, 184–86), cannot be predicted either: coincidental synchronizations of this type are undetermined. Finally, a wide range of strategic interactions have no single predictable outcome. MacIntyre writes about the "game-theoretic character of social life" and mistakenly assumes it to imply *always* indefinite reflexivity, willful misinformation, and a multiplicity of games simultaneously played (1984, 97–98). More vaguely yet more cautiously, Boudon describes the *possibility* of "nonclosed" games as an insurmountable obstacle to social prediction.

Together, these three phenomena of absolute innovation, pure contingency, and nonclosed games give substance to Tocqueville's notion of "chance" and define the limits of determinism in social theory.

Formal Models in Social Theory

The short excursus into the most obvious justification for and limitation of a causal social science has illuminated the last unclear aspect of Tocqueville's reliance on formal models. Their discursive presentation and tentative formalization reflected his awareness at once of the historical nature of social science and of the pitfalls of determinism. With the question of Tocqueville's recurrent use of formal models thus resolved, I turn to address the second issue raised at the outset, whether their potential contribution and possible flaws earn formal models an essential role in social theory as a whole.

Surely there is no need once more to reaffirm the validity of the approach, or to demonstrate anew the possibility of generating knowledge through formal manipulations. The successful identification and specification of various social mechanisms produced thereby has taught us how to detect and rule out fallacious, if intuitive, reasoning by aggregation, and enabled us to better relate individual behavior, institutional settings, and collective outcomes. These achievements have provoked enthusiastic reactions. An authoritative review of

TABLE I
Formal Models in Social Theory

Evaluative principle	Methodological postulates examined and problems generated by them		Missing element
"Truth-Value"	*Model Specifications* Substantive rationality (e.g. value theory)	*Exogenous Preferences* Preference-transformation (e.g. manipulation)	*Interpretive Moment*
"Justice-Value"	*Relativism* Normative evaluation (e.g. choice between ends)	*Rationalism* Preference-formation (e.g. character planning)	*Normative Moment*

political science as a discipline claims the approach constitutes the sole accepted paradigm in the field (Moon, 1975, 195). One of its proponents, even while criticizing its shortcomings, proclaims it unquestionably the best available approach to human behavior generally (Elster, 1979, 65). Such peremptory statements, once the validity and utility of formal models as a fundamental method in social theory are recognized, make it urgent to address their considerable limitations. To ascertain the theoretical boundaries of the method two evaluative principles will be followed: in turn the "truth-value" and the "justice-value" of formal modeling will be examined. (These expressions harbor no metaphysical claims; they simply serve as shorthands for notions of applicability and fruitfulness, and biases and normative implications respectively.) Each such examination will focus on two essential methodological postulates, elaborate their consequences—giving a succinct example of the problems generated in each case—and conclude by pointing out the obvious remedy to these flaws. Table 1 summarizes the procedure and the findings.

Truth-Value

(1) The primary specifications in any formal model of social interaction concern the decision making process of the indi-

vidual actors. Fundamental to this process is the conception of rationality employed. Any abstract definition, however ecumenical its aim, involves the formal theorist in an unpleasant conceptual quagmire—all objectifications of human reasoning processes entail a virtual essentialism (Bourdieu, 1972, 159). Thus the propensity for gain of homo economicus reifies a recent and highly peculiar historical trait (see Polanyi, 1944, 301): as another critic puts it, homo economicus is a universalized homo capitalisticus (Bourdieu, 1984, 34). Even the willful satisfaction of personal preferences, characteristic of homo sociologicus as well, imposes a distorted explanatory scheme on cultures (and individuals) dedicated to their mastery (see Kolm, 1979). Indeed at the extreme, even the minimalist, "procedural" definition of rationality as purely subjective instrumentality (Simon, 1979, 68) universalizes a particular conception of the self as autonomous unit (see Lee, 1959, 128, for the anthropological encounter with a radically different conception). This essential arbitrariness (Hindess, 1977, 158), concealed through habit from the social theorist (Bourdieu, 1972, 173), ultimately distorts the understanding of reality obtained through such models.

A more concrete example of this problem can be given. The moving force behind the deduction for formal modeling, prior to any derivation of resulting causal laws, remains the value theory informing individual choices. In this respect as well, endowing the preferences (utility functions, indifference maps) of the actors in a given model with appropriate substantive content constitutes a formidable challenge (Hardin, 1984, 453). No further elaboration is possible without first confronting this strictly interpretive task. Here, then, intentional interpretation and causal explanation meet, and social theory cannot develop without their cooperation. Clearly a faithful replication of actual individual preferences would remain an asymptotic goal; note then that, at the outset, the purported reliance on strict individual choices proves a chimera (Hardin, 1984, 454). Yet a recourse to a convenient average preference system, allegedly representative of any and all actors, eludes the Charybdis of vacuity only to collide with the Scylla of cultural bias. A debunking of such a cultural practice as the Kula in terms of self-interest, for example, utterly misses its significance. In this specific case, a hermeneutic inquiry would restore the temporal dimension of the practice—the strategically meaningful delays between receiving and giving—dispelling the false impression of an endless yet gratuitous show of kindness (Bourdieu, 1972, 237).

A more recent example, involving less exotic practices, might prove more convincing. In an attempt to apply their methodology to moral philosophy, two theorists formalized a set of distributive principles, calculated the various allocations they would generate in simplified hypothetical cases, and tested the moral intuitions of various subjects regarding the justice of these allocations (Yaari and Bar-Hillel, 1984). The discovery that these intuitions varied widely according to the specific characteristics of the hypothetical cases—their emphases on needs, tastes, or beliefs of the imaginary recipients of the allocations—in spite of the absolute identity of the corresponding mathematical formalizations dramatically illustrates the importance of particular meaning-contexts. (Yaari and Bar-Hillel, 1984, 22, concluded that "a satisfactory theory of distributive justice would have to be endowed with considerable detail and finesse.") As a rule, then, avoiding the hermeneutical confrontation with the particular social setting is bound to encourage a Pygmalion complex in the theorist: a tendency to reshape reality to fit the model.

(2) The dangerous escape of formal theorists from vacuity toward the abstractly universal has a more local but equally misleading counterpart: the methodological postulate on the exogeneity of preferences. Preferences, once specified for a given context, are assumed to remain constant. This artificial severing of preferences from behavior has the merit of easing theoretical deductions; unfortunately, its counterintuitive, indeed counterfactual nature cannot be denied. Unsurprisingly

for a conceptualization adopted uncritically from economic theory, it erases all sociocultural factors influencing the transformation of preferences.

To indicate the gravity of this methodological procedure, I note one crucial consequence. The abstract elimination of preference manipulation constitutes a glaring flaw. Clearly, satisfying consumer or voter wants when these might be the products of corporate or party manipulation would not seem a particularly meritorious goal (Yaari, 1977, 163). The legitimacy of our essential economic and political mechanisms—the market and democratic elections—would thus appear questionable. Yet formal models conceal these problems in assuming the exogenous, independent character of preference, acting in effect as theoretical shields (Attali, 1975, 128). This obvious difficulty has generated an impressive array of criticisms but no satisfying solutions. (To list a few illustrative examples from the last two decades: Schumpeter, 1962, 263; Perroux, 1969, 24ff.; Galbraith, 1971, ch. 6; Lindblom, 1977, ch. 5, 6; March and Olsen, 1984, 736–37.)

It would be premature to rule out the possibility of a formal modeling of various mechanisms of preference transformation, including manipulation. Yet until now, formal theorists and economists willing to confront this issue have been led to admit the necessity of psychological introspection and social inquiry (see, for example, von Weizsacker, 1971, 345; Yaari, 1977, 158; Marshak, 1978, 386; Steedman, 1980, 57–73). Interpretive understanding, once again, would seem a required complement to causal explanation. A single conclusion thus emerges from this examination of the "truth-value" of formal models. At least the vital provision of adequate substantive specifications concerning the decision-making process of the actors, and tentatively the unavoidable confrontation with the phenomenon of preference transformation, depend on a complementary hermeneutical inquiry.

Thus an irreducible interpretive moment in social theory

has been uncovered, proving essential to counteract the limitations of formal modeling (see Dewey, 1954, 160–61, for an early formulation of this essential interpretive core). Consequently all causal laws derived by deduction from such models must remain historical in character (Giddens, 1984, 229), their primary specifications always corresponding to local and specific characterizations of rationality and systems of preferences. Max Weber, who well understood the fundamental interpretive nature of social science, beautifully concluded: "There are sciences to which eternal youth is granted, and the historical disciplines are among them—all those to which the eternally onward flowing stream of culture perpetually brings new problems" (1949, 104).[11] Tocqueville would have subscribed to this conclusion. As the previous examination revealed, his reticence to enunciate general causal laws derived from an acute awareness of the particularity of historical contexts. In fact, Tocqueville's application of the methodology of formal models can be characterized by one distinctive feature: the explicit addition of a first, interpretive step, whereby a value theory suited to the specific social interaction is delineated. For Boudon this refusal to treat preferences as self-evident and independent variables favorably distinguishes Tocqueville's formal models from Marx's (1982, 160–61). Tocqueville recognized the possibility that a system of preferences would not be transparent to the theorists, and thus implicitly acknowledged a distinction between actor and observer of the kind Bourdieu stressed (1972, 159; see also Boudon, 1982, 175–77). His subtle interpretive approach allowed him to perceive the dynamic aspect of preference systems. Tocqueville's hermeneutic method, the logical complement to the methodology of formal models, will constitute the subject of Part II.

---

[11] Mill's conclusion that social laws would forever be "laws of coexistence," historical and particular in their application, seems close to Weber's stand as expressed here (see Brown, 1984, 258–62).

Justice-Value

However, another flaw in the methodology of formal models must be addressed first: its normative bias. Independently of its correctness and applicability, a model carries some moral implications. For Jürgen Habermas, for example, all game-theoretic models exert a subtle technical compulsion on the value systems of the actors. Though allegedly devoid of normative baggage, and hospitable to any and all specifications of individual preferences, they implicitly relativize all such values by comparison to one overriding norm, inherent in the rules of the game: successful self-assertion (Habermas, 1973, 272–73). Habermas's short digression on this subject suffers from some ambivalence. Clearly, his intention could not be to deny the possibility of including altruistic preference systems in game theory. Rather, his criticism might allude to the genuine difficulty, for such models, of conceptualizing radical change: either conversion or willingness to compromise on previously strongly held beliefs.

James March offers a more careful treatment of these issues (1972). Discussing the "justice-value" of social scientific models generally (at least such that attempt to relate individual preferences to social outcomes), March distinguishes between a "relativist" and a "rationalist" bias they embody (1972, 417). The methodology of formal models maintains an Olympian indifference to the preference systems of the actors, and conceptualizes purpose as always antedating action. The reader will have recognized the two methodological postulates already examined for their truth-value; the point of this further discussion, however, is to trace their moral implications.

(1) The methodologically used hospitality of formal models to any system of preferences reveals a retreat from normative evaluation. All values are welcome, for none can be judged. Hume gives a most extreme, albeit illustrative example of this methodical moral relativism, observing that "it is not contrary to reason to prefer the destruction of the whole world

to the scratching of my finger" (*Treatise*, 1978, 416). Such an absolute withdrawal from engagement with normative issues might be temporarily permissible, but remains intolerable in principle. A failure of social theorists to recognize their positive responsibility to confront evaluative questions must be regarded as a breach of duty (Barry and Rae, 1975, 337, 338).

If we push the argument one step further, it can be shown that the relativism of formal models, in a familiar twist, implicitly encourages political conservatism. The abstract equalization of all preferences depoliticizes the social interaction under consideration—*de gustibus non est disputandum*—and all value systems are reduced to mere tastes. Any distinction between such primitive "discrete" wants and "conceptual" preferences, embedded in a wealth of underlying norms, beliefs, and cultural practices, is lost (Sheffrin, 1978). Subtle rationales for alternative values, which could not emerge without public debate and decision, are thereby preempted, while the satisfaction of currently prevailing wants is enshrined (the economists' reification of "consumer sovereignty" being a case in point).

(2) The "rationalist" bias of formal models results from the ill-fated assumption of the exogeneity of preferences. This artificial erasure of any process of goal discovery belies our moral concept of a growing, maturing person. Consider, for example, the following illustrative characterization: "the individual can disappear, provided he leaves us this photograph [the indifference curve] of his tastes" (Pareto, in Hardin, 1984, 463). This "terrible simplification" abstracts from any possibility of personal development: adaptive preferences such as conscious character planning or even learning by doing are excluded. (Elster's discussion of adaptive preferences explicitly excludes character planning and learning by doing, 1983b, 109–24.)

Indeed this failure to recognize a dynamic dimension to preference systems prevents the methodology from addressing a most fundamental normative problem: the choice of ultimate ends. Assuming a genuine absence of developed preferences, and given the obvious need for the selection of a way of life, the only "reasonable" solution offered by such models would seem to be "picking" (see Ullmann-Margalit and Morgenbesser, 1977, for an elaboration of this neglected category of selection). Not only the transformation of preferences, then, but also their original formation cannot be addressed through formal modeling. To the essential debate on ultimate ends they cannot directly contribute.

Albeit following a detour via March's discussion, Habermas's judgment on the poverty of present-day social science thus has been reached: "What was once supposed to comprise the practical efficacy of theory has not fallen prey to methodological prohibitions. The conception of theory as a process of cultivation of the person has become apocryphal" (1972, 304). To give fairness its due, March's subsequent reflections led him as well to call for a reintroduction of moral philosophy into social theory (1978, 601). Surely the very need for such appeals would have appeared incongruous to Tocqueville; the normative implications of his analyses were always at the forefront of his concern, and never remained concealed from the audience he wished to persuade. This normative element of his method, vital for any social theory aiming at practical influence, will constitute the subject of Part III.

The conclusions reached in this chapter can now be recapitulated. Both the initial queries formulated at the outset have been answered in the affirmative. Formal models were a recurrent, intrinsic element of Tocqueville's method, and their potential contribution, especially in light of the possibility of discovering causal mechanisms governing the production of unintended consequences of social action, amply justifies viewing them as an essential component of social theory. Moreover, the examination of the limitations, theoretical and practical, of this methodology—summarized in Table 1—naturally generated a program for further inquiry: social theory, it was seen, must incorporate an additional interpretive and complementary normative element. Each of the following two parts will be devoted to a discussion of one of these elements, in Tocqueville's theoretical practice and in social theory generally.

PART II

HERMENEUTICS

CHAPTER 4

Tocqueville's Hermeneutics:
The Ancient Regime Reexamined

The Old Regime and the French Revolution, though more often read and studied than Tocqueville's neglected *Recollections*, fails today to enjoy as wide an audience as *Democracy in America*. Initially, it had been a much greater publishing success: "The first edition, as big as the first three of *Democracy in America*, was sold out in two months, and that during the doldrums of the summer season" (Herr, 1962, 90). More significantly still, in a field where historical research has persisted for nearly two centuries with unusual—perhaps unparalleled—intensity, Tocqueville's study of the French Revolution "remains required reading for any serious student" (Cannon, 1983, 83), a work considered by the greatest authorities as the finest written on the subject (Lefebvre, 1955, 321; Furet, 1981). In all probability, reflection on the current loss in popularity of this masterpiece would only encourage bitterness and nostalgia; attempting to understand the roots of its successes promises to be a more forward-looking endeavor.

Set back in its original historical context, *The Old Regime and the French Revolution* stands out as a strikingly original work. At a time when remote armchair historiography proved the rule, Tocqueville offered a distillation of painstaking archival research (Furet, 1981, 142). Moreover, braving the uncontested convention of narrative emplotment (viewing history as if it had a plot), Tocqueville chose to draw broad lines of structures and processes. No less disconcerting than the preparation and presentation of the study was its substance: retold as repetition, revolutionary France lost its defining character as a radical break; unintentional consequences of naive or blind policies squarely replaced the much favored conspiratorial theories (Birnbaum, 1970, 88); and, to top it all, a baffling thesis claiming that an improvement of conditions —rather than their deterioration—led to the revolution shattered accepted conceptions of eighteenth-century France and of human rationality alike.

From the opening pages, Tocqueville's favorite tropes indicate his awareness of the work's iconoclastic nature. The phrase "unbeknownst to them," ironically undermining the confident intentionality of human agents, appears in the very first page of the foreword (OC, III, 69), belying the revolutionaries' tremendous effort to transform society. It then provides the substance of chapter 1 (see OC, II, 79), summarizing the contemporaries' blindness to the slow birth and true nature of the revolution. A pendant to this judgment, passing a similar verdict on the errors and ignorance marring later accounts of the process, appears at the bottom of the same first page: "We believe we know very well" eighteenth-century French society (OC, II, 69), Tocqueville observes sarcastically. The second and third chapters, accordingly, are devoted to a deliberately paradoxical account of the revolution's character: contradicting all received wisdom, Tocqueville dismisses as incidental the revolutionary atheism, then deliberately stresses the religious aspect of the French Revolution.

Thus, as these forceful opening chapters undoubtedly demonstrate, Tocqueville consciously sets out to attack the constitutive myth of modern France. Yet significantly, his primary emphasis in these first three pages (which of course were written last) remains the singularity of his method rather than the originality of his conclusions. The book's opening paragraph states the author's rejection of straight narrative, dictated by his main objective: a study of the revolution, not its retelling. The shunning of narrative conventions thus reflects a shift of focus from great actions and events to underlying structures and processes. (For another, not necessarily contradictory reading of this opening statement, see Poggi, 1972, 64.) The next two pages present the author's archival method, the best suited to his main interest: "to penetrate to the heart of this old regime" (OC, II, 70), "its ideas, its passions, its prejudices, its practices" (OC, II, 71). And the foreword appropriately concludes with a paragraph reiterating the exacting care of Tocqueville's research, pointing to the wealth of notes appended to the work as merely a limited selection from the treasures of documentation he unearthed (OC, II, 76; see also 273). I submit Tocqueville's hermeneutic method provides the key to the originality and insightfulness of *The Old Regime and the French Revolution*.

Has this claim, in its suddenly technical formulation, surreptitiously introduced an element foreign to Tocqueville's own thought? After all, no specific mention of interpretive or hermeneutic approaches had been noted earlier, and indeed these concepts do not appear in Tocqueville's methodological self-descriptions. Furthermore, at least according to one current expert, French social theorists of this period as a whole "remained strikingly unimpressed by the soul-searching analyses of philosophical hermeneutics neglecting the presence, across the Rhine, of concerns which the hermeneutic tradition forced social scientists to regard as their own" (Bauman, 1978, 15).

To support my contention in spite of this apparently overwhelming contradictory evidence, a sustained extrapolation from standard definitions of hermeneutics to Tocqueville's classic will be necessary. The definitions used will be taken from the leading authorities in the field, moving from the broader conceptions of philosophical hermeneutics, through more focused treatment of hermeneutics' role in the human sciences, to technically specific applications to historical research. Tocqueville's method will thus be measured against three progressively stricter criteria for hermeneutic inquiry. Surely such a trial, if successfully passed, would amply vindicate a characterization of Tocqueville as a "sociologist" in his approach to social theory. Recalling Barry's description once more, the approach is "discursive, sociological, organismic, literary" (1978, 3). The following examination will sharply highlight these qualities of Tocqueville's work.

Step 1: Hermeneutic Understanding

At the most general level, hermeneutic understanding "commences with the projective anticipation of meaning and proceeds through the dialogical-dialectical mediation of subject and object" (Bleicher, 1980, 3). Insofar as this confrontation and interplay of the interpreter's prejudices and the interpreted testimonies define the hermeneutical "fusion of horizons" (Gadamer, 1982), the forward to *The Old Regime and the French Revolution* evinces the hermeneutic nature of Tocqueville's inquiry. This main exposition of Tocqueville's creative (and recreative) effort clearly delineates three broad stages in that process. Beginning with a candid statement of what he "always had thought" about his subject, Tocqueville proceeds to recall his resolve to "go and question in its grave the France that is no more" (OC, II, 69). Finally, Tocqueville concludes by admitting that studying these archives where he "found the old regime fully alive" (OC, II, 71) forced a refining and rethinking of his initial presuppositions, sometimes against his original expectations:

The more I went forward in this study, I surprised myself in seeing at every moment in France at that time many features which strike one in the France of our days. I found anew in it a multitude of feelings which I had believed born of the Revolution, a multitude of ideas which I had thought till then had come only from it, a thousand habits it alone is considered to have given us; I met everywhere the roots of present-day society deeply emplanted in this old soil. (OC, II, 71)

Yet, if the claim of philosophical hermeneutics to have described the essential structure of any process of understanding is valid, Tocqueville's methodological self-reflection and the revelations above should hardly surprise. Granting the universality of hermeneutics as the ground of any acquisition of knowledge would automatically, and trivially, include Tocqueville's own efforts. To prove that Tocqueville, as the theorist version of Monsieur Jourdain, was practicing hermeneutics unbeknownst to himself, a more methodologically specific definition must be used.

Step 2: Hermeneutics in Human Sciences

One of the seminal statements concerning the centrality of hermeneutics in the human sciences, and probably the most influential Anglo-Saxon reformulation of this thesis, remains Charles Taylor's "Interpretation and the Sciences of Man" (1971). For Taylor hermeneutics' defining characteristic, at once its strength and limitation, is that "its most primitive data would be readings of meanings" (1971, 45). Any theorizing based solely on "brute data"—quantitative statistics, institutional frameworks, legal system—fails on two counts: it hides, hence consecrates the researcher's interpretation of reality, and it eliminates the subject's own interpretation. For Tocqueville, however, these self-interpretations are crucial, being constitutive of the reality he aims to reconstruct and understand. Critics and admirers agree on this point. Irving Zeitlin, in a somewhat dogmatic Marxist reaction, blames Tocqueville for focusing on "the 'superstructure,' the social psychology of men" (1971, 31). In contrast, Jack Lively concludes that "it was in this belief in the leading role of popular mores that the originality of his analysis lay" (1962, 53). Tocqueville's direct testimony, however, brings us even closer to Taylor's own argument. In the following extract from a personal letter, written while at work in the archives of Tours researching *The Old Regime and the French Revolution*, Tocqueville em-

phatically proclaims human self-interpretations to be the core
of any society, hence at once the target of his research and the
aim of his writing:

> You are familiar enough with my ideas to know that I accord institutions
> only a secondary influence over the destiny of men. I would to God
> that I believed more in the omnipotence of institutions! I would have
> higher hopes for our future, because chance could on some given day
> then allow us to fall upon the precious piece of paper that would contain
> the prescription for all our ills, or upon the man who would know the
> prescription. But, alas! It is not so, and I am thoroughly convinced that
> political societies are not what their laws make them but what they
> are prepared in advance to be by the feelings, the beliefs, the ideas, the
> habits of heart and mind of the men who compose them, and what native
> disposition and education made these men to be. If this truth does not
> come forth from all parts of my book, if the book does not cause the
> readers to look constantly within themselves, if it does not indicate at
> every instant, without ever assuming a pedagogical air, what are the
> feelings, the ideas, the customs which alone can lead to public prosperity
> and liberty and what are the vices and errors which on the contrary
> invincibly drive prosperity and liberty away, I shall not have attained the
> principal and, so to speak, the only aim I have in mind. (Herr, 1962,
> 35–36; see also SL, 294)

More specifically still, Taylor describes the inescapable encounter of any interpretive project with the "hermeneutical
circle." Both liberating and entrapping, generating meaning
yet eluding verification, the experience can be described pro-
saically "in terms of part-whole relations": "We are trying to
establish a reading for the whole text, and for this we appeal
to readings of its partial expressions; and yet because we are
dealing with meaning, with making sense, where expressions
only make sense or not in relation to others, the readings of
partial expressions depend on those of others, and ultimately
of the whole" (Taylor, 1971, 6). André Jardin has retrieved a
yet unpublished letter to Freslon, where Tocqueville graphi-
cally describes his own experience with the hermeneutic reconstructive labor: "If I stand too far from the factual details
so as to take in solely the movement of the ideas and senti-

ments ... I remain vague and unfocused; if I come too close to these details, I fall in an immense ocean. ... I have not yet even attained this semi-clarity which enables one to see the countryside and ask the inhabitants for the way" (Jardin, 1984, 486).

One of the most achieved practitioners of this subtle art of finding one's way in a foreign culture, Clifford Geertz, coined the term "thick description" to qualify the patient back and forth weaving of meaning characteristic of the hermeneutic method. Any reader of *The Old Regime and the French Revolution* will recognize the applicability of this characterization to Tocqueville's work; even after the relegation of most of the documentation to the appendix, the text comes together solely as a continuous, harmonious counterpoint of specific, local anecdotes and more tentative wider generalizations. Foreign commentators (notably Arthur Young and Edmund Burke), French leaders (Turgot, Necker), secret reports, and personal diaries all contribute significant touches to this vast canvas; [1] witness, for example, how these combine to recreate the frame of mind of the eighteenth-century French peasant (OC, II, 99–106). Elsewhere, a sweeping statement on the simultaneous decay of feudal institutions throughout Europe draws added illustrative force from a contemporary letter from a German writer, noting the sudden disfavor of all that is old, in particular old furniture (OC, II, 93–94); Tocqueville has a special knack for such revealing prosaic details. Once more, Lively correctly appreciated this skill and perceived its central role in forming Tocqueville's thought: "No one could have been more indefatigable or more skillful in extracting from observations, conversations and documents the hidden assumptions and internal relationships of a society, and his notes and diaries show very clearly that few of his general reflections did not start from some concrete experience" (Lively, 1962, 238).

---

[1] In a letter to Ampère (October 12, 1985; OC, XI, 347), Tocqueville affirms having read and studied most of the many memoirs from the period (see Jardin, 1984, 459).

One might here ponder the nature of the epistemological transition from such concrete experiences, however numerous, to abstract general conclusions. Undoubtedly, this risky process involves eliminating particular differences to achieve an overall view. While the interpreter's art consists in retaining the truly characteristic features, those that render the subject he studies most intelligible and eventually find themselves strengthened in the advent of new evidence, the interpreter's honesty consists in admitting the inescapable partiality of even the most compelling interpretation. Tocqueville, as Chapter 5 will amply document, was well aware of this limitation.

Praising Tocqueville's meticulous research, however admirable in the context of nineteenth-century historiography, would be missing the point: contemporary cliometrics could score higher on this account. What matters most is the guiding intention behind it, the attempts to recreate the web of intersubjective meanings that was the old regime. "You know that it is less the facts that I am looking for in this reading than the traces of the movements of ideas and sentiments," writes Tocqueville to Louis de Kergolay. To succeed in such retracing, "I have up to now found only one way; that is to live, in some manner, each moment of the Revolution with the contemporaries by reading, not what has been said of them since or what they said of themselves since, but what they themselves were saying then, and, as much as possible, by discovering what they were really thinking" (SL, 373). This project, however, cannot be reduced to a naive *verstehen* psychology: with the help of hindsight, Tocqueville can achieve a view of the whole that necessarily remained hidden from the eighteenth-century French, indeed possibly understand their actions better than they could.

Step 3: Hermeneutical Inquiry

To illustrate Tocqueville's grasp of these interpretive subtleties, a comparison between his work and the interpretive categories developed by Emilio Betti will be helpful. Hailed as one of the most sophisticated hermeneutical theorists (see in particular, Bleicher, 1980, 97), Betti has dedicated the bulk of his work to a sustained development of three types of interpretation. The second one, "reproductive interpretation," which aims at communicating a past experience, encompasses the investigation of historical phenomena (Bleicher, 1980, 40, 42). In reproductive interpretation one must pay attention to a crucial distinction between two kinds of sources: "remnants" and "representations." At stake in this distinction is an awareness of the intentions embodied in the sources. While both offer fragments of past life, the latter emerge through the conscious intention of portraying it, hence they already bear an interpretation—possibly biased or distorted—on reaching the would-be interpreter (Bleicher, 1980, 54–55). The letter to Kergolay quoted above clearly distinguished between what the revolution's contemporaries "were saying then," and "what they were really thinking": to retrieve the latter, Tocqueville added, "the minor writings of the time, private correspondence ... are even more effective" (SL, 373). "Remnants," as Tocqueville emphasized, present a privileged, unmediated expression of a way of thinking and being. Yet "representations" can be equally revealing, provided the interpreter dutifully attends to the author's intentions as well as the context.

Consider Tocqueville's careful use of both types of sources. His main primary material, by his own admission, remains throughout *The Old Regime and the French Revolution* the "cahiers." Tocqueville exults in finding this "representation":

The French Revolution is, I believe, the only one at the beginning of which the different classes were able to give separately an authentic testimony of the thoughts they had conceived and to make known the feelings which animated them ... It is the most precious document which remains of old France, and the one which those who want to know what the state of mind of our fathers was at the time the Revolution burst must ceaselessly consult. (OC, II, 293–94)

Could Tocqueville be overly naive in his literal acceptance

of such a conscious, mediated presentation of demands? In
truth, his reading systematically transcends its representational
source, through a restoration of those "diachronic and syn-
chronic developments which have had a bearing on the event
or the motives of the author under consideration" (Bleicher,
1980, 43). Observing that some nobles wish for a distinctive,
external mark to ensure their immediate recognition, Tocqueville interjects: "One could not imagine anything more characteristic than such a demand, or more proper to demonstrate
the perfect similarity which existed already between noble-
man and commoner, in spite of the difference of conditions"
(OC, II, 297; see Stinchcombe, 1978, 44–45, for a related discussion of Tocqueville's use of "effortful distinctions"). Such
postrevolutionary hindsight, available only within an extended historical perspective, contradicts the original beliefs of
the "cahiers'" noble authors, and indeed would have shocked
them. More stunning still would have been a peep at the
"cahiers" written by the other estates, as Tocqueville's reaction
attests:

I read attentively the cahiers written by the three orders . . . I see that here
one demands the changing of a law, there of a custom, and I keep track
of these. I continue thus till the end of this enormous labor, and, when
I come to reunite together all these particular wishes, I perceive with a
kind of terror that what is demanded is the simultaneous and systematic
abolition of all the laws and all the customs currently in practice in the
country. (OC, II, 197)

In this case, the advantage of an unrestricted access to the
entire social scene enables the interpreter to comprehend better the developments. Tocqueville concludes: "I see at once
that at issue will be one of the broader and more dangerous
revolutions which has ever occurred in the world. These who
will be its victims tomorrow know nothing about it" (OC, II,
197). As Bleicher explained, "history is the *locus classicus* for
the possibility of the interpreter understanding the author better than he had understood himself" (1980, 43). At the outset,
in his foreword, Tocqueville simply comments: "I have man-

aged thus to acquire on the old society many notions which the contemporaries did not have; for I had under my eyes what was never revealed to their sight" (OC, II, 71).

Most helpful in achieving this superiority of understanding were of course the various "remnants" Tocqueville so brilliantly gathered and deciphered. Precisely in the lack of conscious, intentional representation, such "traces" (Betti's and Tocqueville's word; see SL, 372) provide "the most genuine and reliable indication of the attitude of their author by allowing safe inference as to the underlying mentality" (Bleicher, 1980, 55). An abundance of examples is available. A particularly striking one, a mundane anecdote succinctly told in a single sentence, will suffice to demonstrate Tocqueville's masterful use of such fragments of culture. In a chapter "How Attempts to Relieve the People Roused It" (OC, II, 226), Tocqueville wishes to explain the seemingly inexplicable inattention of the aristocracy to the people they publicly pitied and openly described as exploited. The priceless piece of gossip brought in to illustrate the situation metaphorically illuminates Tocqueville's thesis: ". . . this recalls a bit the feeling of Madame Duchatelet, who had no qualms, Voltaire's secretary tells us, undressing in front of her helpers, not holding it to be well proved that servants were men" (OC, II, 228). Not only are we at once confronted with this alien, nearly bizarre frame of mind; images of the condemned aristocracy unwittingly undressing itself in front of its potential enemies, glimpses of the coming violation of this delicate, yet degenerate culture—all thoughts Tocqueville certainly harbored—inescapably arise.

Among all the practices interpreters scrutinize in their quest for meaning, linguistic ones are the most pregnant with significance. "Language is constitutive of reality, is essential to its being the kind of reality it is," explains Taylor (1971, 24). The range of human desires, feelings, emotions, "and hence meanings is bound up with the level and type of culture, which in turn is inseparable from the distinctions and categories marked by the language people speak" (Taylor, 1971, 15).

Appropriately, Tocqueville displays a special attentiveness to uses of language and nuances in its variations. In deciphering these practices as well, Tocqueville keeps in mind the crucial distinction between "remnants" and "representations" (without, obviously, referring to these concepts). Limiting constraints of vocabulary are clearly distinguished from affectations of style. Tocqueville's comparative linguistic analysis of the French "gentilhomme" with the English "gentleman," unintentionally reflecting different stratification structures and patterns of class relations, is too familiar to be examined again. Less known is his analysis of the rapid spread of abstract concepts in eighteenth-century political discourse:

> It became filled with general expressions, with abstract terms, with ambitious words, with literary phrases. That style, helped by the political passions which used it, penetrated in all the classes and went down with striking ease to the very last of them. Well before the Revolution, the edicts of King Louis the XVIth spoke of natural law and the rights of man. I find peasants who, in their requests, call their neighbors fellow-citizens . . . (OC, II, 200)

Tocqueville views these practices as a faithful—being unreflective—gauge of the weighty political influence of French intellectuals at that time, the very thesis of the chapter from which this quotation is drawn. Yet his ear remains attuned to any falsity of tone, as when we ironically denounce the vile flattery of some nobles who, hard up for cash, solicit "Monseigneur l'intendant" with seeming humility (OC, II, 137).

Conclusion

Having successfully passed the treble trial of Taylor's criteria, Geertz's characterization, and Betti's categories (augmented with Taylor's clue as to the crucial role of language), Tocqueville's method in *The Old Regime and the French Revolution* undeniably qualifies as hermeneutic. Short of an exhaustive exegesis, more could not be done to prove that much. Yet the exceedingly skeptical reader might still refuse to grant my earlier claim: admitting the sustained presence of a hermeneutic approach does not entail recognizing its paramount importance. In what way does hermeneutics provide the key to the originality and insightfulness of The Old Regime and the French Revolution?

Presuming, at little risk I believe, the probable direction from which such a query could be raised, let me attempt to make my case anew in a different and more straightforward manner. Rather than following Tocqueville's leads expounding on his methodological self-descriptions, one could begin from the modern social scientific judgment on Tocqueville's work, and proceed backward deducing his method. From this nomothetic perspective, The Old Regime and the French Revolution's greatest achievement would be what Boudon (1982, 4) has termed Tocqueville's paradox: the initially puzzling demonstration that a rapid increase in everyone's welfare hastened the outbreak of the French Revolution. Simply stated, my claim is that this main theoretical result, later formalized as "the phenomenon of rising expectations" and modeled as the "J curve," could not have been attained without an inquiry into the historical actors' frame of mind—without a hermeneutical inquiry.

First, the very notion of economic growth in the chaotic mid-eighteenth century French system seemed farfetched to Tocqueville's contemporaries (OC, II, 221). On that account, however, Tocqueville's unprecedented historical research (Cannon, 1980, 75) deserves the praise: such assiduous pursuit of "brute data" suffices to reestablish the facts. Then, more importantly and infinitely more subtly, one needed to reverse all habitual expectations concerning rational action to infer a rising probability of revolt amidst growing prosperity. Nothing short of a hermeneutic inquiry into the actors' interpretations of social reality could ground such a prediction, indeed render it intelligible.[2] Solely a patient immersion

---

[2] Chapter 1 in part II, which opens with a statement emphasizing the reversal of all rational expectations with regard to the Revolution's locus—precisely

in the old regime's culture (Boesche, 1983, 97) could detect the slow transformation of expectations leading to the sudden revolutionary outburst. The analytically minded social scientist rightly might marvel at the elegance of Tocqueville's conclusion. Still, to reformulate this astonishing acceleration of the historical pace we call the French Revolution as the unintended consequence of naively benevolent politics (OC, II, 226–35), Tocqueville had to grasp the simultaneous shifts in self-interpretations accompanying and underlying the political process (see Furet, 1981, 157).[3]

To conclude, then, this examination of Tocqueville's aim, approach, and achievement affirms the key role of hermeneutics in *The Old Regime and the French Revolution*. Tocqueville's principal goal was to reconstruct the web of intersubjective meanings that constituted the old regime. His main method was the careful elucidation of remaining fragments of life, artfully discerning the self-interpretations they harbored. Finally, out of this hermeneutic labor grew his crucial theoretical achievement, the paradoxical thesis of the phenomenon of rising expectations. It remains to be seen whether a broader inference would be valid: was hermeneutics a key element in Tocqueville's method generally?

---

where the yoke of feudalism was comparatively lighter—aptly ends with a lengthy psychological portrait of a typical eighteenth-century French peasant.

[3] Subsequent reformulations of rational behavior in terms of *relative* utility maximization and *adjusting* expectations, as opposed to the static model of exogenous preferences, parasitically depend on Tocqueville's hermeneutic discovery. Furthermore, their application to practical situations necessitates further hermeneutic inquiry in order to determine at what pace and in what manner preference transformation actually takes place in a specific context.

CHAPTER 5

Hermeneutics, in Tocqueville and in Social Theory

This theoretical chapter will elaborate on the local and specific conclusions of the preceding case study. Echoing the concerns of its counterpart in Part I, this chapter addresses the following two questions: Is hermeneutics a recurrent, intrinsic element of Tocqueville's method? Do its potential contributions and possible detractions, on balance, justify viewing it as an essential component of social theory? The obstacles confronting my two affirmative answers mirror those successfully confronted in the case of formal models. For many social theorists, "sociologists" and "economists" alike, hermeneutics still seems a "woolly foreign intrusion to be approached with suspicion" (Bernstein, 1983, 112); while they might agree in recognizing a discursive, historical character to Tocqueville's method, their inclination would be to doubt the coherence and significance of a systematic hermeneutic approach. Furthermore, as mentioned earlier, a number of "sociologically" oriented commentators have denounced Tocqueville's abstract generalizations;[1] indeed none of those professing the exclusive hermeneutic nature of social theory have proclaimed Tocqueville to be an example to behold, much less an impor-

---

[1] See note 1 to Chapter 3, mentioning Pierson (1959), Bradley (1945), and Richter (1970).

tant forerunner.[2] Consequently, a convincing occupation and defense of the still empty intersection of two positive answers to the questions raised requires a further elucidation of the notion of hermeneutics itself, at least as used in this context.

Hermeneutics Generally

Awareness of the suspicious welcome granted hermeneutics, as a primarily Continental approach, prompted me to weave a number of preliminary definitions into the preceding case study. Thus the characteristic "thick description," patiently recreating the internal significance of institutional and behavioral patterns—the submission to the "hermeneutic circle" in order to recapture historically and culturally specific "webs of meanings" should be by now familiar, as concepts and processes alike.

Familiarity, however, implies neither comprehension nor acceptance. The multiplication of superimposed dichotomies designed to distinguish and define the hermeneutic endeavor has generated a great deal of confusion and resistance. Having traveled the road from Dilthey's distinction between *erklären* and *verstehen*, through Windelband's differentiation of "nomothetic" from "ideographic," to Collingwood's severing of causal explanation from intentional interpretation, hermeneutic social theory seemed reduced to a thin, ethereal imaginative gamble—a romantic recapturing of the spirit of a culture ("Erfassung des Geistes," Ast's original concept; see Burke, 1980, 18, and Bauman, 1978, 26). Such a psychologistic characterization, discernible at times even in Weber's habitually more cautious defenses of "interpretative sociology" (see Giddens, 1977, 170), rightly provoked mistrust. Perhaps its most palpably misguided expression is the temptation of some anthro-

---

[2] Here as well as in Chapter 3, I hasten to note one possible exception. Boesche (1983) clearly recognizes the interpretive subtlety of Tocqueville's method; nevertheless, his undoubtedly conscious avoidance of the term "hermeneutics," despite repeated nods in the direction of Dilthey, leads one to conjecture some suspicion toward the method itself.

pologists to go native. Geertz has derided this naive attempt at psychic unity with an alien culture, correctly pointing out the unavoidable reliance on one's own "experience-distant" concepts in order to understand the studied culture's "experience-near" ones (1983, 57). Geertz's discussion, strengthened by illustrations from his own fieldwork, concretely illuminates Gadamer's occasionally nebulous adumbration of the process of "fusion of horizons": hermeneutics neither demands an impossible bracketing of one's concepts and prejudgments nor claims an elusive communion with the studied culture or individual. Indeed even Winch's seemingly moderate dictum that "genuine understanding" necessarily presupposes "the participant's unreflective understanding" (1958, 89) should be faulted on the same grounds. Addressing himself more particularly to the historical reclaiming of one's own culture's past, Gadamer criticizes "the dogmatism of asserting an opposition and separation between the ongoing, natural 'tradition' and the reflective appropriation of it" (1977, 28). The study of past times and distant cultures alike is always already informed by tradition and the theorist's reflective understanding.

While the preceding line of criticism questioned, and curtailed, the possibility of an escape from historically and culturally bound concepts, an equally valid approach would be to doubt its desirability. Setting as the goal for interpretation the unreflective competence of the subjects in the culture studied entails a neglect of the objective conditions in which it is grounded (Bourdieu, 1972). Should it be attainable, complete immersion in the way of life to be interpreted would merely reproduce its participants' naive illusions of spontaneity.

Fortunately, a more mature formulation of hermeneutics' true purpose and role, taking into account these two converging criticisms of its romantic, psychologistic conception, is possible. Giddens's "hermeneutically informed social theory" (1982, 5) consistently pursues both the insight concerning the thoroughly hermeneutic nature of social reality (Gadamer's line), and the recognition of its unconscious and unintentional aspects (Bourdieu's line). Thus reworked, hermeneutics involves both theorist and subjects alike in a dialogical relation of mutual interpretation and reinterpretation—the "double hermeneutics" (Giddens, 1982, 11–14)—while reserving a place for causal explanations of social interactions—the study of unintended consequences (1982, 7, 15). To be sure, neither this reformulation nor my short discussion exhausts either the criticisms leveled against hermeneutics in social theory or the claims raised on its behalf. A more thorough examination can be postponed, for these criticisms do offer sufficient elucidation of the approach to sketch an answer to the first question presented at the outset: Was hermeneutics a recurrent, intrinsic element of Tocqueville's method?

Hermeneutics in Tocqueville

We have seen how, in *The Old Regime and the French Revolution*, Tocqueville's pursuit of the spirit of the old order prompted a hermeneutic investigation of the linguistic structure, the rhetoric, the moral attitude, and the aesthetic sense of prerevolutionary France (see also Gargan, 1963, 336–37). Similar interests dictate a similar method in the *Recollections*. In two opening paragraphs, the character of the work and its intent are specified: the *Recollections* offer a participant-observer account, aimed at faithfully mirroring the physiognomy of the ages (R, 3–4). Tocqueville's occasional emendations and suppressions have been noted earlier, yet the overall candor of his analyses amply justified the careful delay in publication (the *Recollections* were published posthumously). As for the restriction to firsthand account, Tocqueville rarely strays away from his self-imposed rule, and offers his apologies and justifications when he does (R, 142). Such restraint, however, should not be confused with a refusal to reach behind appearances and observed phenomena: Tocqueville (R, 4) explicitly sets out "to uncover the secret motives that made us act." Thus alongside the causal explanations such as the formal models uncovered earlier (in chapter 2), intentional interpretations would be attempted.

Best remembered among these are Tocqueville's psychological portraits of important French leaders. Tocqueville's capsule descriptions are deservedly famous for their vibrant recapturing of essential characteristics: origins, tastes, language, and appearance might be noted, but always the idiosyncratic way of thinking and its moral and political implications are granted the most detailed attention (see, e.g., R, 6–7 on Louis-Philippe; 107ff on Lamartine; 202–4 on Louis-Napoleon). Each portrait carefully restores the historical context for this individual character, uncovering the deeper reasons for its emergence into prominence at that particular juncture: individual psychology remains at the service of a broader hermeneutical inquiry. Admittedly, little commentary can be adduced to validate this conception of the work, the project being a fiercely private one. Yet in another context (discussing his intelligence techniques as foreign minister), Tocqueville explains that "when one wants to judge or anticipate the great movements of parties" (the *Recollections* clearly belonging to the former kind of endeavor), one must turn to "the look of the whole country and knowledge of its needs, passions and ideas" (R, 206).

To illuminate this economic, emotional, and intellectual world Tocqueville resorts to a technique that served him well in *The Old Regime and the French Revolution*: illustration through telling anecdotes. Both the process of interpretation and the process of demonstration, the confrontation with the subject as well as with the reader, relied heavily on Tocqueville's eye for significant details. One of his rare departures from the self-imposed restriction to firsthand accounts draws its justification from the fact that the story told, though "very trivial," "wonderfully illustrates the character of that time" (R, 143). Child-servants, in their characteristically careless expressions, reveal their hope that after the revolution, they "will be eating the chicken wings" and wearing "the lovely silk dresses." Tocqueville rhetorically asks: "What better illustration of the spirit of the time could one find than this childish story of naive cupidity?" His commentary, moreover, does not neglect to point out the master's attitude, carefully concealing his having heard the children and dismissing them only after the insurrection's defeat: in such manner the microsocial episode illuminates the whole social scene. Similarly, a seemingly inconsequential incident, Tocqueville's encounter with a stubborn old woman pushing a vegetable barrow, suddenly assumes a broad political significance. Her violent reaction, from Tocqueville's perspective, reflects "demagogic passions and the fury of civil war" (R, 145). Here as well a methodological observation accompanies the account: "If one pays attention and notices such things, they provide a very reliable index of the general state of mind." Clearly one could reverse the tables on the interpreter, and question his description of the peasant's "frightful and hideous expression" (R, 145) or his reference to the child-servants as "monkeys" (R, 143). Still, the richness of his thick descriptions remains undeniable, and to some commentators, Tocqueville's essential achievement. It is "as portraitist or landscapist of the democratic society of his day that he earned a lasting place in the literature of social philosophy," writes Nisbet (1976, 110), who grants Tocqueville's portraits "a central place in creating the vision of the masses in European writing."

Perhaps the best description of French lower-class types in the *Recollections* remains Tocqueville's juxtaposition of his two household subordinates. Though they were actual, historical individuals, their preserved anonymity (only one first name is mentioned) ensures their perception as types: biographical material deserves recollection only for its broad historical import. Thus Tocqueville's concierge comes to represent the worst aspect of lower-class behavior, from drunkenness to wife beating, from mere envy to murderous schemes (or at least boasting of them). To Tocqueville, in a particularly vindictive mood, such is the "socialist by temperament" (R, 155).

Eugene the manservant, in contrast, stands for the traditional, loyal and obedient lower class valet, content with his lot and devoted to the existing order. Such an attitude draws great praise from Tocqueville, who describes it as an unconscious following of philosophic precepts, the maintenance of "that happy balance between power and wants" (R, 157). Once more, however, most telling are the interactions between master and servant, the hostility and suspicion between Tocqueville and his morally, politically, and economically estranged concierge as opposed to the friendly if paternalistic attitude toward the respectful manservant. It would be hard to surmise if Tocqueville would have drawn the same conclusions from these interactions as the contemporary reader might; still, their willful juxtaposition reflects his consciousness of the emblematic importance of these episodes.

A lengthy analysis in *Democracy in America*, the work to which I now turn, testifies to Tocqueville's awareness of the representative character of such authority patterns. The transformation in the relations between master and servant with the transition to democracy was judged sufficiently illustrative of that new regime for Tocqueville to devote to it an entire chapter (vol. 2, pt. III, ch. 5). In this more analytical mode, the divorce from firsthand experience is more accentuated, yet the same categories reappear. Crucial to Tocqueville's examination, as the two poles of a continuum on which democratic authority patterns will be located, are two types of servants in aristocracies: the mean and servile "lackeys" (DA, 574), and the "trusted retainers" (DA, 576), the loyal "valets." Clearly these categories, perhaps unconsciously, governed Tocqueville's subsequent reflections in the *Recollections*. His study of democratic mores, however, indicates the development of a mid-range position, between the absolute loyalty resting on self-identification and the anger of humiliation: master and servant in democracy "are neither scornful nor angry, and look at each other without pride or humility" (DA, 577). Here the early Tocqueville provides a sociological gloss on the late one. His calm analysis lucidly diagnoses the likely revolutionary juncture between aristocratic and democratic authority patterns, the "moment of hesitation between the aristocratic conception of subjection and the democratic conception of obedience" (DA, 579). No wonder this superb hermeneutic illumination of the historical transformation of authority patterns inspired subsequent analyses of the process (see e.g. Bendix, 1964). Tocqueville's masterful stroke was to center on the most inherently hierarchic relationship, that between master and servant, in order to underscore the profound effect of the spirit of equality (Manent, 1982, 51).

The techniques employed to bring out this profound effect will be familiar from the examination of *The Old Regime and the French Revolution*. To capture the gradual softening of mores in democracy Tocqueville relies on personal letters, truthful "remnants" of aristocratic attitudes. Madame de Sévigné's correspondence with her daughter, particularly her chillingly casual description of torture on wheel, brings home better than the most scholarly study the aristocratic incapacity of conceiving "what it was like to suffer if one were not of noble birth" (DA, 564; recall the undressing duchess in *The Old Regime and the French Revolution*). To indicate the equal dignity of all labor, and the absence of social distinction on such basis, Tocqueville relies on linguistic practices, faithful "traces" of democratic conceptions. While part of the available vocabulary, the word "peasant" does not appear in the effective vocabulary: "The word is unused because the idea is unknown; the ignorance of primitive times, rural simplicity, and rustic villages have not been preserved with them, and they [the Americans] have no idea of the values and the vices or the rude habits and the naive graces of newborn civilization" (DA, 303).

Tocqueville's preoccupation with such "remnants" stems from the same hermeneutic interests already expressed in *The Old Regime and the French Revolution*: the importance of mores, "a universal truth" that "occupies the central position in my thoughts" (DA, 308). Indeed the most extensive definition of the term, as Tocqueville understands it, can be found in a passage of *Democracy in America*: "I here mean the term 'mores' (moeurs) to have its original Latin meaning; I mean it to apply not only to 'moeurs' in the strict sense, which might be called the habits of the heart, but also to the different notions possessed by men, the various opinions current among them, and the sum of ideas that shape mental habits" (DA, 287). For Melvin Richter, this conscious broadening of the term, however thoughtful and explicit, amounts to careless management of Montesquieu's much more precise category, a sloppiness characteristic of Tocqueville's "habitual forgetfulness" (1970, 90–91). Yet Tocqueville's explanation shows concern for both linguistic roots and current technical usage, and he clearly states the reasons for his operational definition. His wish is "to cover the sum of the moral and intellectual dispositions of men in society" (DA, 305 n8). This grand ambition, coupled with the relative paucity of factual observations in Tocqueville's two-volume masterpiece, probably stands at the origins of the many scholarly criticisms of Tocqueville's method.

Even Mayer's eulogistic commendation of Tocqueville's "remarkable power of abstraction" implicitly suggests a flaw in the process of generalization. For Tocqueville, it seemed history and facts served mainly as convenient canvas on which to elaborate bold ideas (Mayer, 1966, 66). Other commentators discuss this procedure in more critical terms, their accusations taking either one of two forms: Tocqueville was guilty either of hasty inductive inferences from a highly selective data base (Bradley, 1945, xciv), or of facile deductions from a priori generalizations (Richter, 1970, 71). Either an ideal type of democracy was constructed too quickly and rigidly, or, still worse, facts played but an intellectually and chronologically secondary role as support for flimsy principles (Birnbaum,

1970, 32, 33).[3] In both cases the back and forth between ob-servation and generalization appears short-circuited, a criti-cism first raised by Sainte-Beuve (1860) and made famous by Pierson (1959).

Yet other commentators, notably Boesche, claim Tocque-ville rooted his analysis in thorough examinations of particular cultures, consciously avoiding "the pitfalls of grand theories" (Boesche, 1983, 96). Indeed Riesman concluded that Tocque-ville was more of an interpreter than a thinker, an ethnogra-pher rather than a theorist (1961, 175–76). A clue to a solution of this conflict of interpretations can be found in more detailed examinations of Tocqueville's actual methodological practice.

Drescher carefully noted how Tocqueville always strove "to convert specific observations into the broadest generalities": as a result conclusions would frequently fluctuate whenever new situations needed to be confronted (1964, 26). When con-ceptual schemes obviously distorted newly available evidence, they had to yield (Drescher, 1964, 72–73). Schleifer's (1980) invaluable analysis of the making of *Democracy in America*, by reaching behind the process of demonstration—Tocque-ville's published text—fully recovered this process of interpre-tation. Reflection, personal experience, and earlier readings dictated general principles, and guided the search for sup-porting evidence (Schleifer, 1980, 9). Often, though, Tocque-ville's expectations were frustrated: even a subject "already resolved in so many ways could present itself" to him under a new guise (quoted in Schleifer, 1980, 72). Consequently prin-ciples had to be adjusted or abandoned (e.g. Schleifer, 1980, 46). Schleifer's analysis meticulously illustrates the continuous spiral of "anticipations" and "disappointments" until "fulfill-ment" be reached, the sustained hermeneutic circle governing Tocqueville's inquiry.

To those unfamiliar with or hostile to the hermeneutic jar-

---

[3] Birnbaum himself, having echoed these views and supported them with (se-lective) evidence from Tocqueville's correspondence, finally retreats to a much milder—if less documented—view (see 1970, 36).

gon, the terms in quotation marks above will seem pompous and fuzzy substitutes for the simpler "hypothesis," "falsification," and "verification." However, as defined for example by Husserl, the types of feedback associated with "disappointment" and "fulfillment" differ in kind from the typical scientific confrontation with evidence. Rather than providing a simple affirmation or denial of a specific state of affairs predicted by a hypothesis, and thus confirming or falsifying it, the encounter between the interpreter's horizon and particular aspects of the culture studied might enrich or transform the former without ever forcing its abandonment entirely (see, e.g., Buck, 1978, 34–39). This peculiar sturdiness of the broad informing conceptions initiating the hermeneutic inquiry in part explains the criticisms raised by so many commentators against Tocqueville's allegedly a priori method.

A complementary explanation is unwittingly offered in another estimate of Tocqueville's achievement: "Rarely does de Tocqueville actually report what he saw and heard in America; rather he reports his own inferences and generalizations from what he saw and heard" (Costner, 1976, 419). The paucity of "hard data" in *Democracy in America* led critics to assume a dearth of factual research, a misguided view (and a hasty deduction par excellence) that only thorough research of the type Schleifer undertook could refute. A quick glance at Tocqueville's own notes from his American journey will suffice to support that more generous view of Tocqueville's method without simply leaning on Schleifer's work.

Paul Lambert White, the first scholar to study these notes, mistakenly thought of them as innocent marginalia. This artificial divorce of Tocqueville the "solemn commentator" on institutions from Tocqueville the "amused recorder" of the lighter side of life precludes a grasp of the manifold reach of Tocqueville's hermeneutic effort. Not only can sources for many of Tocqueville's telling anecdotes in *Democracy in America* be traced back to these systematic notes (e.g. DA, III, 218), but even some of his most famous analyses can be found, in various stages of elaboration, in these pages (e.g. the comparison between Ohio and Kentucky, DA, 47). It is hard to see how a reader of both could fail to recognize the intimate link between the book and the notebooks. For that very reason, the latter remain invaluable, as they throw a bright light on Tocqueville's method. Without the benefit of any of the following technical categories, Tocqueville deployed an impressive panoply of research methods: ethnographic accounts (e.g. DA, 187, 188), participant-observations (e.g. DA, 342–43), systematic surveys (e.g. DA, 309–11, noted also by Jardin, 1984, 147), and lengthy, carefully prepared interviews (e.g. DA, 280), all balanced by an unusual attention to details of verbal nuances (e.g. DA, 33 nl).[4] This intensive and extensive effort to recover the self-interpretation of Americans, their conceptions of themselves and their society, led Tocqueville himself to some measure of self-irony. About his discussion with Beaumont concerning the best schedule to adopt in their brief visit to New Orleans, Tocqueville wrote: "We made an infinite number of classifications. We created principles of observation, then we made deductions from our principles, then deductions from our deductions; we discussed, classified, unclassified for an hour and noon was smiling upon us when we finally adopted the following plan..." (DA, 379). Such are not the methods of a casual commentator. Neither are the feelings expressed in the following letter those of a dogmatic, predisposed theorist. Once appearances are perceived, writes Tocqueville to his friend and advisor, Louis de Kergolay, "when one wants to penetrate a little further, one finds real difficulties that were not expected, one proceeds with a discouraging slowness, and doubts seem to grow the more one progresses. I feel at this moment that my head is a chaos into which a throng of contradicting notions are pell-mell making their way" (SL, 46).

---

[4] The crucial importance Tocqueville granted such field research methods can be gauged by his resolute abandonment of an extensively prepared study of India, once plans for touring the country collapsed (see Jardin, 1984, 325).

Boesche's sustained reflections on Tocqueville's singular theoretical achievements led him to affirm that "no other political thinker in his century so completely immersed himself in all aspects of his political and social world" (1983, 97). This conclusion remains undeniable, yet stands in need of two important qualifications. Both hinge on the relation between Tocqueville's and Dilthey's methods, noted and discussed by Boesche as well (1983, 85, 88). Was Dilthey's enthusiastic endorsement of Tocqueville (see ch. 1 above) indicative of an identity of aims and methods? An examination of this question will take us through an important detour, delineating both the place of interpretation and the danger of subjectivism in social theory. As the reader will promptly note, and might have already inferred, these observations will mirror the reflections on the place of causality and the danger of determinism in Chapter 2, hence the quicker pace adopted here.

The Place of Interpretation

Once more, any discussion of ontological groundings will be resolutely avoided. In the case of a hermeneutic social theory as well, the attempt to anchor the methodology in a firm grasp of "ultimate reality" must be self-defeating.[5] No such access to an unmediated reality is intelligible, let alone practicable, according to philosophical hermeneutics. As Gadamer is fond of repeating, "all thinking about language is already once again drawn back into language" (1977, 62).

Yet the reclaiming of a central role for intentional interpretation in social theory must be welcomed. Causal mechanisms, at the very least given the present state of neurophysiological knowledge, cannot provide an explanation for most human action. Formal deductions, governing a prospective praxeology or a "logic of preferences" fail as well (see von Wright's repudiation of his earlier attempts in that direction,

---

[5] " 'The world' is either the purely vacuous notion of the ineffable cause of sense and goal of intellect, or else a name for the objects that inquiry at the moment is leaving alone" (Rorty, 1972, 663).

1983, vii–ix and passim). To put the point simply and briefly, our satisfaction at having understood an action is predicated on a reconstruction of individual decisions within an intelligible framework of beliefs. Such a reconstruction presumes either a priori knowledge of the applicable framework, or a thick description aimed at recapturing the singular "web of meanings" within which the action is inscribed.

Boesche correctly identified the intimate connection between Tocqueville's "mores" and Dilthey's "web of meanings" (1983, 85), yet, significantly, stopped short of explicitly qualifying Tocqueville's method as hermeneutic. Given the nature of Dilthey's contribution to social theory, and the aim and character of Tocqueville's work as revealed by this examination, this qualification cannot be avoided. As Boesche himself amply documented, Tocqueville was aware, at least within his own work, of the important distinction between *erklären* and *verstehen* (Boesch, 1983, 85; see also DA, 214–15), and considered his analysis complete only once a comprehensive grasp of the "spirit" of the culture he studied had been achieved. Consequently the particular research techniques he favored anticipated those suggested by contemporary "qualitative," "interpretive" social theorists, spanning the continuum from anthropological fieldwork to textual exegesis. The previous case study of *The Old Regime and the French Revolution* as well as the preceding examination of *Democracy in America* and the *Recollections* documented this foreshadowing of Geertz's, Betti's, Taylor's, and Husserl's methodological categories in Tocqueville's actual practice. One can only hope that the evident success of the latter will prompt a greater respect for the concerns and suggestions embodied in the former.

The Danger of Subjectivism

While refraining from explicit references to hermeneutics, Boesche's parallel between Tocqueville and Dilthey emphasized a shared romanticism. Eager to inscribe Tocqueville within the French nineteenth-century tradition, Boesche one-sidedly characterized Tocqueville's interpretive inquiry as a psychologistic one (1983, 88). The fallacies embodied in such an approach have been pointed out earlier in this chapter: duplicating an actor's inner feelings is impossible, and moreover insufficient from the perspective of social theory. Was Tocqueville naive enough to espouse such an elusive goal, and complacent enough to satisfy himself with a participant's understanding of the culture he studied?

Both the previous case study of *The Old Regime and the French Revolution* and the preceding examination of *Democracy in America* and the *Recollections* have carefully noted Tocqueville's departure from a naive psychologistic inquiry. Admittedly Tocqueville always strove to recreate a culture's spirit, and maybe even overestimated his capability to recapture the actors' true feelings and motivations. Nevertheless, his goal throughout remained to achieve a better understanding —more comprehensive and more penetrating—of the society he studied than the one available to its participants. Tocqueville never doubted, for good reasons, that his analyses provided fresh insights into the ancient regime and the American democracy: he understood both systems better than their members ever could.

The question of subjectivism offers a second, related aspect. Considered from the perspective of the subjects interpreted, rather than the interpreter, Dilthey's method leads to a misguided creationism, a quasi-existentialist belief in the spontaneous formation of meaning systems by the actors within them. Certainly Dilthey's (and Winch's) radical denial of the applicability of causal mechanisms in the explanation of human affairs would seem to imply an overly exalted view of the freedom of human creative powers. Two fallacies can be pointed out in this case as well, both bearing on the all-too-rigid distinction between human and natural sciences. (1) Both endeavors share a residual interpretive core, as recent philosophy of science has demonstrated (see Hesse, 1974), and (2) both legitimately include causal mechanisms in their overall explanatory schemes (as Chapter 3 emphasized).

On this second point at least, the only one concerning us in this investigation of the limitations of a naive subjectivism, Tocqueville's position has been made clear. While resisting Gobineau's mechanistic schemes (see Chapter 3), Tocqueville nevertheless derided "aristocratic" historians who failed to see beyond the intentions and actions of social actors (see Chapter 2), not to mention educational utopians who put great trust in mere ideas, these "vaporings of litterateurs" (AR, 160). More positively, the particular attention he brought to bear on the problem of unintended consequences as well as his repeated reliance on formal models amply illustrate Tocqueville's grasp of the role of causal mechanisms in human affairs.

Summing up this short digression, I conclude that Tocqueville's method, like Dilthey's, was hermeneutic—aimed at the understanding of shared cultural meanings. Yet, unlike (at least the early) Dilthey, Tocqueville proposed to transcend the participants' self-interpretation, and resolutely enlisted causal explanations in his methodological efforts. The question concerning Tocqueville's sustained reliance on a hermeneutic method has thus been answered affirmatively, generating in the process a further clue as to the possible limitations of such a method for social theory as a whole. I now turn to an examination of the second question raised at the outset, addressing the role of hermeneutics in social theory generally.

Hermeneutics in Social Theory

With the rich contribution of the hermeneutic method to social theory highlighted by Tocqueville's example, little need remains for commending it further. One could also cite enthusiastic endorsements of the method as the main if not the sole approach in social theory. "In contrast to the incapacity of a science which remains within the accepted categories, a hermeneutical science of man which has a place for a study of intersubjective meaning can at least begin to explore fruitful avenues" (Taylor, 1971, 42). Such peremptory statements, once the validity and utility of hermeneutics as a fundamental method in social theory is recognized, make it urgent to address its considerable limitations.

Despite the structural similarity of this examination to the one regarding formal models in Chapter 3, the different nature of the subject matter lends itself to a different treatment. Debates on interpretive social theory have been internal to a great extent, evolving historically along party lines drawn in fin-de-siècle Germany. The remarkable paucity of sustained external critical analysis reflects the theoretical disdain of Continental approaches by the positivist scientific orthodoxy. Consequently this examination will be divided between an assessment of the *Methodenstreit* (the conflict on method) and a review of the *Werturteilstreit* (the conflict on value judgments). Within the hermeneutic tradition, these famous debates most closely duplicate the concern with "truth-value" and "justice-value" that occupied the examination in Chapter 3. Here as well, a table recapitulating the findings, translated into the language of these more familiar categories, will be offered at the conclusion of the analysis.

Methodenstreit

The clash of competing approaches to social theory, initially centered on the nature of economics, was originally embodied in an 1880 debate between C. Menger and G. Schmoller. At issue was the validity of two modes of theorizing, one exact in form and nomothetic in aim, the other historical in character and ideographic in goal. Sparing the reader the endless vagaries of this dispute, I enter the matter directly via one of its more recent and familiar avatars.

(1) Winch's (1958) post-Wittgensteinian idea of social science affirmed the unique character of each "form of life," de-

manding unconditional empathy from the theorist eager for true understanding. The most vigorous repudiation of both this affirmation and the consequent demand has been formulated by Gellner (1970, 1975), a rare instance of direct external criticism worthy of consideration. Taken straightforwardly, the methodological postulate of the extreme endogeneity of each culture would seem to refute the possibility of translation, thereby entailing a form of cultural solipsism: only from within a culture could one understand it, and the sole correct understanding would be the native's own, as embodied in the culture's language and practices. Clearly, then, the possibility of cross-cultural generalizations, of any higher-level theoretical synthesis, would be forgone. Indeed, even the humbler goal of retrieving and communicating alternative "forms of life" would seem endangered.

Thus queried, hermeneutic theorists such as Winch and Geertz replied by admitting the retreat from grand theory (Geertz, 1973, 26), yet salvaging the more modest ambition. Translation was not impossible—after all, such was the achievement of practicing cultural interpreters—but rather difficult and forever tentative. Hence the "wisdom" (see Winch, 1972, 42) of other cultures was still accessible. Thus, for Geertz, "the essential vocation of interpretive anthropology is not to answer our deepest question, but to make available to us answers that others, guarding other sheep in other valleys, have given, and thus to include them in the consultable record of what man has said" (1973, 30).

(2) Not content with this readjustment of goals, Gellner's critique proceeded to challenge hermeneutic inquiry further. Another, related methodological postulate was deemed insufficient, namely the adoption of a "principle of invariably benevolent interpretation" (Gellner, 1975, 152). Two levels of criticism are combined in this attack on methodological empathy: a contrast to actual theoretical practice, and a subtle demonstration of theoretical inadequacy (both appear in Gellner, 1970). Not only do interpreters necessarily translate into

their own terms, hence possibly distort, the phenomena and events recorded; more problematically, excessive interpretive charity would blind them to a whole range of social behavior, involving the (intentional and unintentional) use of ambiguity, absurdity, and self-contradiction. A priori, the principle of benevolence in interpretation would decree the absolute coherence and consistency of any cultural system—understood in terms of *our* logical criteria of course. Moreover, the instrumental nature of the ambiguity of certain terms, hidden by this a priori assumption, would not reveal itself to the investigator (see Gellner, 1970, 41–46). Finally, the possibility of social change following an eventual recovery of such conceptual inconsistencies would remain obscure as well to the hermeneutic investigator (1970, 47).

Gellner's (1975) dissection of the possible flaws in a thoroughly contextualist interpretation illuminates the broader accusation of idealism he levels against hermeneutics. Surely the pitfalls of a social theory guided by the motto of *credo quia absurdum* are evident. Resistance to such sensible criticism derives from a deeper motivation, often unacknowledged— the fear of naturalistic, "meaningless" explanations of human behavior. Defending a rigid contextualism and demanding an absolute attention to ostensible cultural meanings as shared in a given culture express a rejection of mechanistic, causal explanations (1975, 130–32). This protective attitude toward an exclusively "anthropomorphic image of man" (Gellner's paradoxical yet telling phrase), however, dictates not only the abandonment of general theory (1), but also the curtailment of our understanding of any particular culture (2).

Thus the need for a broader methodology in social theory becomes obvious. Not only the phenomenon of unintended consequences and the possible mechanisms of unconscious behavior, but also the very attempt to generalize and reach broader conclusions, as well as the effort to penetrate the practices of the culture studied, require transcending the strictures of a rigid hermeneutic approach. An additional explanatory moment, complementing the essential hermeneutic immersion, must be part of the method of social theory.

Werturteilstreit

Another flawed aspect of hermeneutic methodology needs to be addressed as well: its normative implications. The infamous Popper-Adorno debate on positivism (*Positivismus-streit*), occasioned by the meeting of the German Sociological Association in Tübingen in 1961, renewed a much earlier dispute on the role of value judgments in social sciences (*Wertur-teilstreit*), begun in earnest at the Vienna general meeting of the Verein für Sozialpolitik, in 1909 (see Adorno et al., 1976, xxix). The common core of these debates was a questioning of the ends embodied in the methods of social theory. Burdening this chapter with a reconstruction of Sombart's and Knapp's arguments at the turn of the century would be pointless, and the single, unfortunate consensus reached by the debaters in the 1960's remains a bitter agreement on the ultimate barrenness of their lengthy confrontation. However, particularly given the dearth of sustained criticism of hermeneutics outside the Continental tradition, much can be learned from the more recent contributors to the aforementioned debate—specifically from the exchange between Gadamer and Habermas.

(1) At issue, then, is the normative import of hermeneutics; what, in a parallel analysis of formal models in Chapter 3, was termed the "justice-value" of the methodology. Habermas (see esp. 1972) recasts the argument as an examination of the interests motivating the adoption of a particular method.[6] A single-minded preoccupation with nomological laws—the hallmark of positivism, indeed of "scientism" that regards science as the sole way to knowledge—betrays a simpleminded concern with technical mastery. In contrast, a hermeneutic social theory brings in a crucial attention to purpose and meaning, a "prac-

---

[6] I do not agree with Habermas's typology of interests, a theoretical move generating many difficulties (for one recent criticism, see Elster, 1983a, 16): my aim is only to present and incorporate his criticism of hermeneutics.

tical" interest. Habermas thus welcomes this addition, recognizing the central role of language as the medium of intersubjectivity, constitutive both of our social world and of our self-understanding. Self and society are possible only in terms of commonly shared concepts; this main hermeneutic tenet, Gadamer's essential message (as well as the later Wittgenstein's), is accepted by Habermas.

Yet, even with the inclusion of hermeneutics, social theory still lacks the embodiment of a third, crucial kind of interest: the quest for emancipation that fuels criticism. For Habermas, beyond nomological laws and hermeneutical queries, social theory needs a critique of ideology.

Gadamer, in the most developed philosophical elaboration of hermeneutics (1982), asserts that all knowledge is generated by tradition, indeed is possible only within a tradition. Meaning emerges only within the horizons of a reappropriated given culture, that is an assimilated given language. (The already examined methodological postulate of the endogeneity of forms of life reemerges here in an epistemological guise.) Such a theoretical posture, Habermas retorts, smacks of conservatism: it prostrates social theory in a permanent, crippling bow to the authority of tradition. Gadamer's rehabilitation of informed prejudgment as the key controlling access to knowledge all too easily slides into a glorification of prejudices. Consequently, his "idealism of linguisticality" (Gadamer, 1977, 29) exhausts itself in mere cultural transmission, ignoring the concrete realities of work and action shaping society—hence remaining powerless, unable to bring change. Habermas's earlier writings already pointed out that the medium of intersubjectivity, language, was simultaneously "a medium of domination and social power" (1967, 178). Perhaps a more biting, and certainly a more extended, gloss on this argument has been offered in the work of Foucault. His efforts have persistently illuminated the forever present interplay between knowledge and power, between relations of meaning in discourse (the focus of hermeneutics) and the power relations in society (the ultimate concern of a critical social theory). Hermeneutics' systematic disregard of this dialectic is the target of Habermas's criticism.

In sum, a social hermeneutics content with its humble encompassment within tradition abandons all hope of enlightenment. By definition, it cannot recognize a possible state of "false consciousness," or debunk an eventual ideology, however politically dangerous and theoretically misleading such commonly accepted (self-)delusions could potentially be. Having sealed itself in the steel cocoon of language, hermeneutics thus has betrayed enlightenment: it stands convicted of irrationality.

(2) Habermas's resolve not to abdicate the right, in principle, to submit tradition to scrutiny has a close counterpart in the Anglo-Saxon philosophical world. Albeit directed at another personal target and much less receptive to hermeneutics generally, Gellner's strictures against the "new idealism" (1975, 129–56) in social sciences identify another, related weakness of hermeneutic social theory. Habermas uncovers, in Gadamer's temporalization of Heidegger's reflection on "language as the house of being," a cultural conservatism unamenable to rational criticism. Gellner, for his part, follows Winch's spatialization of Wittgenstein's reflection on "language-games" as "forms of life" to its equally sheltered terminus: a profound cultural relativism. Governing history, hermeneutics rules as a jealous mistress; serving anthropology, it proves a promiscuous lover.

As is often the case, these two misfortunes are not unrelated. The theoretical self-confinement within the prison house of language, which forced the unquestioning acceptance of the authority of one's tradition, precludes by extension the development of any cross-cultural principles of selection (Gellner, 1975, 138–39). Piously attuned to the echoing meanings constituting the form of life it studies, a hermeneutic endeavor has no recourse to any external standards. It thus perforce adopts a stance of moral neutrality. Once more, a paralyzing, epistemologically motivated suspension of judgment spells the abdication of criticism. On this wider, cross-cultural scale, however, the retreat from the normative translates into a complacent relativism. Enclosed in their idiosyncratic cultures, even the most morally repugnant or aggressively minded forms of life must be viewed and treated with equanimity. Hermeneutics, thus, stands convicted of relativism.

This verdict as well, though Gellner (unlike Habermas) raises it in his eagerness to reject hermeneutics and return to a strictly nomological social science, underscores the need for a third, normative moment in social theory. To safeguard the possibility of internal and external criticism alike—the debunking of "false consciousness" as well as the arbitration among "forms of life"—an explicit normative stand must be taken. Neither the search for nomological laws nor the quest for intersubjective meanings satisfies this demand. The countervailing analysis of Chapter 3 should make it clear that hermeneutics' incipient irrationalism does not constitute an antidote to the excessive rationalism of formal models (indeed both tend to reinforce a conservative bias), and both methods altogether cannot escape relativism, be it cultural or individual.

In conclusion, a short recapitulation of this chapter's findings is in order. The results of this last section are encapsulated in Table 2, a table structurally similar to Table 1 above; a juxtaposition of the two tables should facilitate a comparison of the findings of Chapter 3 and the present chapter. Hermeneutics has been shown to be a central, permanent part of Tocqueville's method, and proven a vitally useful element in social theory as a whole. On the negative side, we have seen how the methodological postulates of hermeneutics, the endogeneity of "forms of life" and interpretive empathy, led to solipsism and idealism respectively. Those flaws called for explanation, enabling theoretical generalizations and the detection of ambiguities (or even absurdities). On the level of this "truth-value"

TABLE 2
Hermeneutics in Social Theory

Evaluative principle	Methodological postulates examined and problems generated by them		Missing element
"Truth-Value"	*Endogenous* *"Forms of Life"* Solipsism (e.g. generalizations)	*Empathy* Idealism (e.g. absurdity, ambiguity)	*Explanatory Moment*
"Justice-Value"	*Irrationalism* Authority above emancipation (e.g. "false consciousness," ideology)	*Relativism* Abdication of judgment (e.g. arbitration among "forms of life," external standards)	*Normative Moment*

analysis, formal models and hermeneutics plainly complement one another, the latter supplying the former with its sorely missed interpretive moment.

Yet on the level of a "justice-value" analysis, hermeneutics' irrationalism and relativism merely compound the problems uncovered in the previous examination of formal models, the latter's inherent rationalism and relativism. More than a back and forth movement between formal models and hermeneutics would be needed to rehabilitate social theory from a normative standpoint.[7] To the examination of this missing third normative element of social theory I now turn.

---

[7] This solution, in widely divergent formulations, seems to be common to Habermas and Gellner; it will be addressed in my conclusion (Chapter 8). On its own, my analysis at this point has made obvious the need for a radically different, third normative element.

PART III

NORMATIVE STAND

CHAPTER 6

Tocqueville's Normative Stand: *Democracy in America* Reexamined

Widely read, and still more extensively quoted (often in distorting fashion), *Democracy in America* has retained the classic status it so rapidly gained a century and a half ago. Turning to it demands some justification, a promise to the reader that well-covered grounds will not be trod once more. Accordingly, this case study focuses on an issue rarely (and only tangentially) addressed by commentators: Tocqueville's normative stand. Refining this focus slightly, I will be concerned here with the relation between Tocqueville's analysis and the values he espouses, not with the particular substantive values he advocates. Thus conceived, the question of Tocqueville's normative stand is methodological, not (at least not directly) political.

To begin locating Tocqueville's position on this question, it will be helpful to draw inspiration from his own comparative techniques and fashion an abstract dichotomy of alternative ideal types. Less charitable readers might view those proposed here as straw men; however, the intention at this point remains solely to provide a first exploratory approximation toward a definition of Tocqueville's stand. Theoretical subtleties are not eschewed, but postponed for the following chapter. To sharpen the contrast, and cover a maximum expanse of ground on the continuum between the ideal types, the normative attitudes opposed will be the "classical (political) philosophy" stand versus the "modern (social) scientific" approach.

In this schematic characterization, the first ideal type denotes a conception of the analysis of society as embedded in and a continuation of ethics, while the second embodies a willful striving for normative neutrality. Support for this necessarily arbitrary dichotomy can be found in Jürgen Habermas's contrast of "the classical doctrine of Politics in relation to social philosophy" (1973, 41–81), though two departures from his analysis should be noted at the outset. What Habermas calls "social philosophy" here is labeled "social science," the distinction being merely semantic, but nevertheless potentially confusing. More profoundly, Habermas generously endows his classical ideal type with a praiseworthy respect for the inherent uncertainties and plasticity of things human. Drawing mainly on a self-serving, though quite plausible if not unchallengeable interpretation of Aristotle, Habermas characterizes the classical approach as rejecting the quest for absolute *epistēmē* in favor of a more flexible *phronēsis*. In light of what appears to me a far more convincing reading of "the tradition" (elaborated in the writings of Nietzsche, Heidegger, Derrida, and Rorty, to call on but a few references), the "classical" approach as defined here partakes of the "quest for certainty," and aims to attain an absolute knowledge valid across time and space, periods and cultures. These two caveats aside, Habermas's analysis will provide the background for this examination: the normative yet overly subjective classical stand will be contrasted with a more rigorously objective if devoid of value orientation modern approach (1973, 44).

Though these ideal types might appear rigidly bare, it should be mentioned that the "modern" one encompasses at least two important variants, which together cover much of the contemporary social science literature. Both the crude *wertfrei* methodological decree—a delusion at best, a deception at worst—and the naive commitment first to make explicit one's values then to proceed with an "objective" analysis, should be included under the "modern" rubric. Both participate in the "cult of neutrality" (Taylor, 1967, 48) and consequently assume the separate ontological status of facts and values. Where, then, in relation to these stands of subjective commitment and detached objectivity, have commentators located Tocqueville? To convincingly demonstrate that the proper answer is "everywhere," an illustrative sample of learned statements on the question will be offered. Starting with the first, classical model, and somewhat less recent interpretation, consider Harold Laski's conclusion: "But what remains outstanding in Tocqueville as an historian is the intensity of feeling his work displays. Behind the assumption of calm objectivity it is not difficult to discover the real passion by which it is informed" (1950, 111). Closer to us, Edward T. Gargan went even further in the same direction. His remark on Tocqueville's normative stand nicely captures the impetus behind the classical approach: "Tocqueville did not believe that a passionate involvement in the destiny of one's nation presumed an impediment to the attainment of truth in the study of its fate. On the contrary, to Tocqueville, such a commitment alone provided the force to give direction to one's life" (1955, x). In the same vein, yet worth mentioning for their negative attitude toward Tocqueville's stand as characterized above, are Peter Gay's comments, notably the following backhanded compliment in a footnote on *The Old Regime and the French Revolution*: "That his book remains interesting and valuable is a tribute to his style and to his penetration in areas in which he was not blinded by his preconceptions" (1959, 8n13).

Precisely the opposite conclusion, exonerating Tocqueville of any exclusive and excessive passion or prejudice, was reached earlier by Albert Salomon: "He was intellectually and morally so detached that he understood in its logical development the historical process and the final defeat of his class, and therefore he regarded the outcome as providential" (1935, 408). More recently, another recognized authority, Jack

Lively, seconded this characterization to the point of making
it a key to Tocqueville's achievement as a theorist: "These
Ishmael-like qualities, his critical, aloof and independent
standpoint, ill-fitted him for political success, but they helped
to make him one of the greatest political observers and thinkers of the nineteenth century" (1962, 5). In addition to these
strikingly opposite judgments, and to be expected given such
contrasts, one can also identify somewhat baffling middle-of-
the-road positions. Carl Becker, pondering "Why De Tocqueville wrote *Democracy in America*," describes Tocqueville as
a would-be objective analyst ultimately committed to some
higher political values. Indeed, claims Becker, "it would be a
great mistake to suppose that Tocqueville was sufficiently objective not to care whether democracy was beneficial or harm-
ful, to suppose that he was primarily interested in the social
revolution as a phenomenon to be intellectually apprehended"
(1958, 168–69). Drawing closer in time once more, we find
Pierre Birnbaum lending a crowning touch to this confusion.
His Tocqueville, in puzzling fashion, appears as a would-be
classical student of society—"one cannot separate, in examining Tocqueville's work, the rigor of the scientist from the conviction of the political man" (1970, 7)—ultimately achieving
an unexpected impartiality: "It seems, however, that his sociological methods escape, in spite of all, that kind of influence"
(1970, 16).

   This confusing array of contrasting judgment was not raised
to be derided; rather, given the undeniable competence of
these respected commentators, the aim was to underline the
complexity of the question and the need for a more refined
answer. (Marvin Zetterbaum's nuanced characterization of
Tocqueville's stand will be addressed in the following chapter.)
It would also be prudent, beyond even the worthy considerations of fairness to the authors quoted, to admit at the outset
that Tocqueville's own comments lend themselves quite easily
to different interpretations. Solemn inaugural pledges of impartiality (DA, 20, 418) and casual endorsements of political

(e.g. DA, 600) as well as aesthetic (e.g. DA, 606) normative positions coexist in seeming peace and harmony throughout *Democracy in America*. Still, to succumb immediately to the conclusion that Tocqueville simply was inconsistent would be a facile retreat from interpretation. Judging from the legacy of previous commentators, the more interesting possibility that Tocqueville's normative stand eludes conventional categories seems likely, and deserves to be examined first.

Indeed a comparison with the ideal types defined earlier strengthens the suspicion that Tocqueville fashioned himself a particular stand. No elaborate analysis is needed either, because a rapid process of elimination conveniently offers itself. In reference to the interpretation of the tradition adopted here (as distinguished from Habermas's), the claim of the classical approach to generate absolute knowledge had been stressed. Confident in the universal nature of the moral order constituting their starting points, classical philosophers—again, one should emphasize, for the most part—presented their conclusions as *sub specie aeternitatis*. Notwithstanding their radically different attitude to the moral order—in fact, in their eyes, because of it—social scientists partake of the same "quest for certainty." Their attempts to attain or fashion an Archimedean point aim at generating universally valid conclusions as well. Thus both normative stands, in their shared aspiration to emulate a divine all-encompassing perspective, stamp their products with the same epistemological status. That stamp—"this conclusion applies everywhere and forever"—is missing from Tocqueville's works.

One little-noticed chapter in *Democracy in America* addresses itself to this epistemological issue (vol. 2, pt. I, ch. 3). Tocqueville's investigation of the status of general laws hinges on the philosophical problem of the One and the Many, the question of identity and difference. First, the divine perspective is succinctly described: "The Deity does not view the human race collectively. With one glance He sees every human being separately and sees in each the resemblance that makes him like his fellows and the differences which isolate him from them" (DA, 437). Consequently, being able to hold simultaneously the One and the Many in sight, God needs no generalizations. Human intelligence, however, inevitably fails to grasp and retain the infinity of details constituting reality. Any attempt to examine and judge all particular cases ultimately leads to losing sight of the whole, hence to blindness. This imperfection alone forces a resort to generalizations. Thus, concludes Tocqueville, "general ideas do not bear witness to the power of human intelligence but rather to its inadequacy ... General ideas have the excellent quality, that they permit human minds to pass judgment quickly on a great number of things; but the conceptions they convey are always incomplete, and what is gained in extent is always lost in exactitude" (DA, 437). These lucid propositions call for no elaboration. Two qualifications, however, are in order. Cautiously restricting the range of this conclusion, one must note that Tocqueville consistently links his discussion to human affairs, never mentioning the natural sciences and their subject matter. Then, enlarging somewhat the scope of Tocqueville's analysis, it should be remembered that in all probability Tocqueville did not believe in God (I will return in more detail to this controversial issue in the next chapter), whose anthropomorphic nature as a seeing and thinking function thus merely provided here a convenient metaphor. The perspective presented by Tocqueville as "divine" should be understood therefore as a forever elusive epistemological ideal. Its very unattainable character dictates a skeptical, even sarcastic attitude toward all claims to absolute knowledge: "I wake every morning to be told that some general and eternal law of which I have never heard before has just been discovered. No writer, however second-rate, is satisfied with an essay revealing truths applicable to one great kingdom, and he remains dissatisfied with himself if his theme does not embrace the whole of mankind" (DA, 438). The moderation of aspirations strongly suggested at the end of this quotation applies to Tocqueville's own work.

An objection to this characterization of Tocqueville might be expected. Addressing it at once will prove worthwhile insofar as this preemptive move uncovers two important features of Tocqueville's normative stand. Certainly, Tocqueville has not been thought of before as a "postmodernist," weary of any and all "metanarratives," to borrow Lyotard's terms (1979; see, however, Brunius's *Alexis de Tocqueville: The Sociological Aesthetician*, 1960, 16, 60, in which Tocqueville is described as a "cultural relativist"). After all, did he not at times claim to reach universalizable conclusions? That such claims are occasionally made by Tocqueville is undeniable. In examining them, however, one can distinguish between three kinds of seeming lapses into absolutism, in ascending order of seriousness.

Most innocuous are those lapses that seem little more than figures of speech, generalizations vague enough to be acceptable to all. To state that "the importance of mores is a universal truth to which study and experience continually bring us back" (DA, 308), given the resolutely undefined character of the extent of this "importance" as well as the mechanism ensuring its diffusion, is not to claim the discovery of a universal law. Rather, Tocqueville wishes to acknowledge the crucial role of mores in his thought, as the next sentence attests: "I feel it occupies the central position in my thoughts; all my ideas come back to it in the end" (DA, 308). Most of Tocqueville's comments about "human nature" can be similarly explained.

Thus few would dispute the assertion that "egoism is a vice as old as the world" (DA, 507), particularly as Tocqueville neither attributes that vice to all men and women generally, nor claims it to be ineradicable regardless of education and social forms. Tocqueville's observations about human "perfectibility," the faculty of self-improvement distinguishing mankind as a species from animals, appear equally moderate. Once more, essential parameters such as pace, direction, and ultimate goal(s) of the presumed human progress are left decisively vague; indeed, Tocqueville ridicules the propensity of aristocratic culture to believe it has drawn close to absolute perfection. The passage deserves quoting, as it reaffirms Tocqueville's distrust of absolute claims: "So they do not imagine that they have arrived at the supreme good or absolute truth (what man or what people has ever been so mad as to imagine that?), but they like to persuade themselves that they have pretty nearly reached the degree of greatness and knowledge which our imperfect nature allows" (DA, 453). Even such toned-down pretensions are judged presumptuous by Tocqueville.

A more problematic lapse into absolutism takes the form of an invocation of some "natural order" in human affairs, possibly impervious to changing mores. Tocqueville's treatment of sexual equality seems the most prominent case in point. Thundering against new-fangled feminist demands for absolute equality between the sexes, especially in the social and political realm, Tocqueville declares: "It is easy to see that the sort of equality forced on both sexes degrades them both, and that so coarse a jumble of nature's work could produce nothing but feeble men and unseemly women" (DA, 601). In contrast, great praise is bestowed on the American way of achieving equality through the separation of masculine and feminine spheres of action, and in particular the maintenance of what Tocqueville unabashedly terms "the social inferiority of woman" (DA, 603). Unquestionably, Tocqueville's theoretical defense of this position centers on an appeal to "Nature" (see Morton, 1984, 322), "which created such great differences between physical and moral constitution of men and women" (DA, 601). At least the second part of this appeal commits the absolutist sin, reifying a social conception (however prevalent historically) into a natural law. To my mind, however, Tocqueville is simply resorting to the most powerful rhetorical trope available. Determined to stem this new wave of equality, which he fears threatens the moral foundations of society (of which women in their private role are the main guarantors), Tocqueville risks a translation from biological to moral spheres he knows to be slippery. Evidence of this awareness can be found in the opening paragraph of this chapter: "I have shown how democracy destroys or modifies those various inequalities which are in origin social. But is that the end of the matter? May it not ultimately come to change the great inequality between man and woman *which has up till now seemed based on the eternal foundations of nature?*" (DA, 600; emphasis added). Clearly, then, the human understanding of these "eternal foundations" might be changing. Additional evidence for the rhetorical nature of Tocqueville's claims in this discussion can be adduced from its concluding paragraph: "And now that I come near the end of this book in which I have recorded so many considerable achievements of the Americans, if anyone asks me what I think the chief cause of the extraordinary prosperity and growing power of this nation, I should answer that it is due to the superiority of their women" (DA, 603). This oddly inflated statement, conspicuously absent from Tocqueville's other summary conclusions throughout *Democracy in America*, testifies to the strong rhetorical flavor of his discussion of sexual equality. While the seeming lapse into absolutism thus has become intelligible, a lesson to be remembered has been gained from this examination: the powerful normative commitment informing Tocqueville's analysis.

The most problematic of Tocqueville's apparent lapses into absolutism must now be confronted. Both volumes of *Democracy in America* contain arguments about justice that clearly seem to evoke a set of universal moral standards. Earlier on, troubled by the boundless power of the voting majority, Tocqueville sought to devise a legitimate escape route: "When I refuse to obey an unjust law, I by no means deny the majority's right to give orders; I only appeal from the sovereignty of the people to the sovereignty of the human race" (DA, 250–51). Much later, reflecting on the shifting and contradictory character of conceptions of honor, Tocqueville wished to retain some permanent criteria to judge them by: "The prescriptions of honor will therefore always be less numerous among a people not divided into castes than among any other. If ever there come to be nations in which it is hard to discover a trace of class distinctions, honor will then be limited to a few precepts, and these precepts will draw continually closer to the moral laws accepted by humanity in general" (DA, 623). This passage, in fact, has recently been criticized for its facile "universalism" (Walzer, 1983, 276; see also Lively, 1962, 166). Can these arguments be reconciled with the characterization of Tocqueville as an antiabsolutist?

Note, first, Tocqueville's careful wording of the latter claim, which suggests that the universality of certain moral laws derives from generalized acceptance rather than from higher grounds. In fact, Tocqueville's first argument, defending civil disobedience, remains cast entirely in this immanent democratic mode. Its starting point is the seeming contradiction between Tocqueville's acceptance of majority will as the fount of political power and his rejection of the majority's right to do everything it pleases. To maintain coherently both positions, Tocqueville simply enlarges the scope of his theory of legitimacy: "A nation is like a jury entrusted to represent universal society and to apply the justice which is its law" (DA, 250). Accordingly, the "universal justice" to which he appeals retains a statistical and democratic character, rather than assuming a transcendental one. Indeed Tocqueville describes it as a law "made, or at least adopted" (note his preferred wording) by the majority of mankind (DA, 250). Finally, Tocqueville never specifies the substantive content of that universal standard: when already alluded to, absolute principles remain cautiously empty.

Tocqueville's most sustained effort to define such universal moral standards, at the beginning of his second argument, the discussion of honor, illustrates this caution: "There are some universal and permanent needs of mankind on which moral laws are based; if they are broken all men everywhere at all times have connected notions of guilt and shame with the breach. *To do wrong* means to disregard them, *to do right* to obey them" (DA, 616–17). Two caveats promptly follow this already softened and diffuse moral absolutism. Specifically, "special needs" evolving from particular circumstances "modify the way of looking at human behavior and the value attributed thereto"—indeed possibly making as radical a transgression as homicide "excusable or even honorable" (DA, 617). And generally, Tocqueville characteristically remarks, "nothing is so unproductive for the human mind as an abstract idea. So I hasten to consider the facts" (DA, 617). Fittingly, in the following consideration of specific examples, Tocqueville's historical perspective effectively neutralizes any inclination toward moral absolutism he might have harbored instinctively. Two passages exhibiting this tension can be identified. Judging actions "exclusively with reference to the person who did them or suffered from them," peremptorily declares Tocqueville, "is repugnant to the universal conscience of mankind" (DA, 616). Yet this outraged reaction merely punctuates an explanation of how this allegedly "universal" principle by no means was widely accepted, much less consistently applied in feudal society. Similarly, Tocqueville's claim that the love of money stands condemned by "the universal conscience of mankind" simply heightens our awareness of the powerful shaping of influence of the "particular and momentary need" of a community, as in expanding Jacksonian America "no stigma attaches" to that lowly passion (DA, 621). Hence the phrase "the universal conscience of mankind" should be read as a rhetorical trope indicating the passion of Tocqueville's normative commitment rather than as a claim to have uncovered a moral absolute.

All three types of Tocqueville's seeming lapses into absolutism can thus be explained without much damage to his characterization as a postmodernist *avant la lettre*. Should this reading remain unconvincing, a more minimal claim could be made: though striving to avoid absolutism, Tocqueville failed to refrain from unfortunate lapses and hurtful inconsistencies.

Few thinkers, if any, are free of such defaults, and Tocqueville's effort remains his distinctive achievement from this perspective. Granting this restrained characterization suffices for my argument.

Still, his discussion of the sociology of values, with which this examination has concluded, naturally leads to a more aggressive defense of that characterization. As Karl Mannheim —surely an authority on the matter—noted, Tocqueville was a founding father of the sociology of knowledge (1953, 83). This oft-neglected aspect of Tocqueville's achievement has received the more extended treatment it deserves in Birnbaum's monograph (1970, ch. 6; an earlier little noted, and somewhat cursory, discussion can be found in Brunius, 1960). Its import for this analysis should be evident: no consistent sociologist of knowledge, as Marx as well as Mannheim quickly learned, can easily fashion a secured Archimedean point from which to profess *sub specie aeternitatis* conclusions. The insight into the unavoidable cultural anchoring of values, beliefs, fiction, and research alike that provides the driving force behind sociology of knowledge proves fatal to absolutist aspirations in both ethics and epistemology. That insight, of course, sparks most of Tocqueville's incisive observations on democratic culture throughout volume 2 of *Democracy in America*. One could plausibly argue that Tocqueville in some respects pursues it more deeply and more consistently than either Marx or Mannheim. Both ultimately succumb to the temptation of artificially cleansing one elected social stratum (be it the proletariat or the intelligentsia), thereby securing a robust launching pad for universalist conclusions. In retrospect Tocqueville's analysis seems more sophisticated: admitting the inevitability of prejudice offers but a starting point before celebrating its invaluability. Tocqueville's thesis is simple—received ideas and dogmatic beliefs are a vital necessity for community (DA, 433–34), and no less indispensable for the individual (DA, 434). His straightforward language could only suffer from paraphrases:

If man had to prove for himself all the truths of which he makes use every day, he would never come to an end of it. He would wear himself out proving preliminary points and make no progress. Since life is too short for such a course and human faculties are too limited, man has to accept as certain a whole heap of facts and opinions which he has neither leisure nor power to examine and verify for himself, things which cleverer men than he have discovered and which the crowd accepts. On that foundation he then builds the house of his own thoughts. He does not act so from any conscious choice, for the inflexible laws of his existence compel him to behave like that. (DA, 434)

A skeptical reader might dismiss the last line's allusion to the unintentional, unconscious nature of the ideological penetration of individual thought—to refer anachronistically to Freudian and Marxian vocabulary—on the ground of the thoroughly voluntaristic tone of the rest of the passage. Still, two points should be noted: the whole passage, except that last line, describes a hypothetical counterfactual, and even in voluntaristic terms the demonstration of the inescapable historical grounding of individual thought remains irrefutable. No one, not even the greatest philosopher, can escape its logic.[1] Yet, argues Tocqueville, this seeming predicament should be welcomed as "desirable as well as necessary": "It is true that any man accepting any opinion on trust from another puts his mind in bondage. But it is a salutary bondage, which allows him to make good use of freedom" (DA, 434). Only the unassuming lucidity of Tocqueville's formulation can explain why this grasp of the benefits of prejudice had to await Gadamer's belated (and occasionally cumbersome) analysis (1982).[2] It must be concluded that Tocqueville assumed a thoroughly historicist attitude.

[1] An astute explanation of lawyers' acquired distaste for revolution and popular behavior, which also mentions their potentially leading role in the new democratic nation (DA, 264), could perhaps be read as a reflexive sociology of values —a self-reflective application of the approach only perfunctorily undertaken by Marx and Mannheim. (See also SL, 34–35; Tocqueville, of course, was a lawyer by training.)

[2] "I have never had much taste for metaphysics, perhaps because I never seriously devoted myself to it, and because it has always seemed to me that good sense led to the goal it contemplates as well" (Tocqueville to Corcelle, October 16, 1855; SL, 320).

The result of the comparison to the "classical" and "modern" ideal types can now be summarized. As both share absolutist claims, neither fits Tocqueville's normative stand. His reluctance to provide final blueprints, resounding answers, cover-all solutions might be disappointing to some and admirable to others. Yet, whatever the judgment, his determination to qualify his suggestion and admit his informed bias distinguishes him from most of his predecessors and successors alike. That substantive departure reflects the crucial impact of his rejection of absolutism, and testifies to its uniqueness.

Moreover, another crucial feature of Tocqueville's particular stand has been noted: his powerful normative commitment. Considered in isolation, this aspect links Tocqueville to the classical tradition. Yet his historicist awareness forces him to reflect on his prejudices, to recognize the inevitability of residual biases, and thus to resist their reification into absolute principles. In that fashion Tocqueville strives toward the elusive blend evoked by Habermas in the analysis quoted earlier: "Providing practical orientation about what is right and just in a given situation— ... without relinquishing ... the rigor of scientific knowledge" (1973, 44). Little wonder, then, that this particular stand confused commentators content to rely on conventional categories. In Tocqueville's approach, "objectivity" does not mean value-free, strictly descriptive analysis; "normative" does not imply a lapse into merely subjective evaluations;[3] and "scientific knowledge" does not spell the attainment of alleged absolutes. Tocqueville offers a more rigorously objective, normative analysis, while eschewing absolute dictates.

This carefully drawn conclusion further complicates the task of characterizing Tocqueville's normative stand: any attitude eluding conventional categories challenges positive description. In Tocqueville's case, moreover, a puzzling blend of pos-

---

[3] Only Costner (1976) seems to have reached a similar conclusion (see, in particular, 412, 423), though he trivialized the meaning of impartiality for Tocqueville ("simply being as honest as possible with one's data"; DA, 424).

sibly contradictory tendencies must be reconstructed in intelligible and coherent fashion. Can one shun absolutism and avoid subjectivism in an analysis deeply informed by a resolute normative stand? Conversely, can one maintain normative commitment—overcoming a relativist ("anything goes") apathy—in an analysis informed by penetrating insight into the intellectual feebleness and ideological embeddedness of all thought (see Tocqueville's arguments on generalizations and sociology of knowledge, respectively)? Though, logically, normative commitment and epistemological humility need not be mutually exclusive, a psychological tension between the two subsists. Method being our concern, precisely this question of the translation of Tocqueville's theoretically complex stand into practice must be addressed. In a writer not given to detailed methodological elaborations, the slightest hints might be of great value. One might thus be allowed to begin the positive reconstruction of Tocqueville's stand with a short digression into strategically located metaphors.

Notwithstanding his earlier strictures, Tocqueville ends *Democracy in America* with a proclamation of his attempt to emulate "the Almighty and Eternal Being, whose gaze of necessity includes the whole of created things": "I therefore do all I can to enter into understanding of this divine view of the world and strive from thence to consider and judge the affairs of men" (DA, 704). What does this effort to achieve an ideal he has defined as unattainable entail? Restored to the context of *Democracy in America*'s conclusion, the divine analogy serves to underline Tocqueville's endeavor to shed his original (aristocratic) values in favor of alternative (democratic) ones, a normative transition of the greatest import he wishes to make explicit (DA, 704–5; this move illustrates the important theme of "value trade-off," to which this analysis will later return). Significantly, however, the conclusion of the first volume presented a similar image, though divested of any divine connotation. In a celebrated metaphor, Tocqueville envisioned himself as "a traveler who has gone out beyond the walls of some vast city and gone up a neighboring hill" (DA, 408), thus achieving a unique perspective. What could the methodological equivalent of this metaphorical ascent be? In this case, of course, Tocqueville alludes to his endeavor to summarize his survey and venture some broad conclusions. Still, if one is willing to generalize as well, and abstract momentarily from specific contexts, both Tocqueville's concluding images center on one main aspect of his relation to his subject: distance. Distance, I propose, is the essence of Tocqueville's normative stand.

This claim can be reformulated more systematically. Tocqueville's stand is characterized by a methodological distance—intentionally achieved—from his subject, a distance that provides the key to his puzzling blend of normative commitment and epistemological humility. Confirming this thesis thus calls for a demonstration of Tocqueville's conscious efforts to distance himself from his subject, as well as for an explanation of the beneficial role of these efforts in balancing Tocqueville's precarious position.

Distance emerges embodied in Tocqueville's title: *Democracy in America* presents a subject first, then its merely temporary location (for Tocqueville, in contrast to his eighteenth-century predecessors, the New World illustrates the future of the Old, not its original past; DA, 18). Admittedly, the disjunction in *Democracy in America* between locus and object of study has become an interpretive commonplace, at least since Sainte-Beuve's comment on the second volume: "America, in the near decade since he has left it is nothing more than a pretext for the author; it is but a figurehead, and it is to the modern societies generally, and to France as much as to America that he addresses himself" (1860, 15, 95). While Sainte-Beuve's tone was critical, J. P. Mayer's later emphasized both the general theoretical aim of Tocqueville's indirect approach—the structural study of a new political order (Mayer, 1966, 29)— and its specific political motivation: the drawing of practical lessons for French developments (1966, 5). Granting the latter interpretation, perhaps more still can be made of Tocqueville's decision. First, though in light of the broad theoretical aim Tocqueville's move might seem unsurprising, with regard to the main political goal it appears somewhat circuitous. Turning one's sight away to better comprehend (and possibly influence) one's subject would not be the obvious, impulsive choice. Furthermore, a restoration of the historical context eliminates the false aura of naturalness we would tend to attribute to Tocqueville's move, even in relation to his general theoretical aim. Though from our vantage point Jacksonian America might offer the choice locale for the study of democracy in vivo in mid-nineteenth century, such was not the consensus in Tocqueville's own circle. Intellectually Great Britain was considered the traditional alternative in political typologies, at least from Montesquieu on. Politically, moreover, supporters of America came mostly from the Freemason and republican ranks (Furet, 1984, 226). Tocqueville himself was an aristocrat of conservative-liberal leanings, and a fervent admirer of Montesquieu. Significantly, no mention of America (though numerous of England) can be found in his correspondence prior to his departure. Finally, to ward off the cynics, it might be worth noting that the official titles and mission Tocqueville and Beaumont succeeded in wresting from the French authorities provided no financial retribution. Being thus strikingly original, given both Tocqueville's theoretical and political goals, and consequently highly conscious, his decision to study and write on America must have resulted from deeper, yet to be uncovered reasons.

In truth, Tocqueville's political and theoretical objectives had been made explicit at the outset. Curiosity, however legitimate, did not motivate his travels. Rather, he "sought there lessons from which we might profit" (DA, 18): "I admit that I saw in America more than America; it was the shape of democracy itself which I sought, its inclinations, character, prejudices, and passions; I wanted to understand it so as at least to know what we have to fear or hope therefrom" (DA, 19). If such was the proclaimed intent of the first, more conventionally descriptive volume, one can safely infer as much regarding the second. Indeed a fragment entitled "Explanation of the Object of the Work" observed: "The first book more American than democratic. This one more democratic than American" (Schleifer, 1980, 19). Criticisms of Tocqueville's selective survey of America, in particular his relative inattention to the South and overemphasis on the Northeast, thus never should have been raised. Tocqueville openly indicated his reasons for disregarding the Southern states (low social and anti-intellectual origins, slavery), as well as his particular interest in New England (middle-class, Puritan origins and a full-blown democratic system) (see DA, 34–35, 39, 43). Clearly, his quest was for a typical democratic environment, closer and more representative of the Old World. Once more, then, the question arises: why go so far, with England across the Channel?

A helpful structure for elaborating an answer can be borrowed from Gunnar Myrdal's monograph on *Objectivity in Social Research* (1969): its schematic nature makes it convenient for that purpose. Aware of the impossibility of a "disinterested" social science (1969, 55, 74), Myrdal redefines "The Problem" of the social theorist's normative stand around three crucial axes. "How," asks Myrdal, "can the student of social problems liberate himself" from:

(1) the powerful heritage of earlier writings in his field of inquiry, ordinarily containing normative and teleological notions;

(2) the influences of the entire cultural, social economic, and political milieu of the society where he lives, works, and earns his living and his status; and

(3) the influence stemming from his own personality, as molded not only by tradition and environment but also by his individual history, constitution, and inclinations? (Myrdal, 1969, 3–4)

The emphatic language of these questions underscores their rhetorical nature, the necessarily asymptotic character of the aspirations they embody. Yet they present a valuable checklist, indicating sensitive junctures between value orientations and theoretical analysis. Precisely these three junctures are more carefully articulated, intentionally as will be shown, as a result of the distance Tocqueville established from his subject.

(1) Recalling the originality of Tocqueville's research location, one realizes that his decision left him to confront a relatively uncluttered literary heritage. Unlike the much analyzed (and much celebrated) British system, American politics and culture had not yet been fitted to some accepted conceptual mold, and still awaited a "definitive" treatment. These circumstances encouraged the kind of fresh, unencumbered thinking Tocqueville wished to engage in. As for the few works already published on his subject, they were resolutely disregarded. James T. Schleifer has underlined, sometimes critically, Tocqueville's desire to isolate himself from other writings on his subject, in order "to know his own mind and to maintain his intellectual integrity and originality" (Schleifer, 1980, 82). As an example Schleifer discussed the case of Poussin's important work *Les Travaux d'améliorations intérieures*: "As is well-known, Tocqueville insisted on insulating his own ideas and reactions from the influence of other recent European, and especially French, travelers to the United States. Poussin's status as a fellow foreign visitor necessarily condemned the work to inattention" (Schleifer, 1980, 78).

(2) Nothing better than the abrupt transition from Old to New World could force to the surface unrecognized assumptions and implicit beliefs. The contrast in social scenery, from personal manners to political organization, could not have been starker (as long, obviously, as one wished to study modern societies). From Tocqueville's perspective America was an inverting mirror, where one's own features stood out in their conspicuous absence: a land without a feudal past, skipping revolutionary stages, devoid of any aristocracy—indeed with little history; an unlimited land of many races, materially prosperous and intellectually limited—indeed with little high culture. America was the Other, the ideal locus for insightful comparisons, for self-discovery. Such comparative strategies

were of course an essential part of Tocqueville's methodological arsenal. Furet (1984) has described the tridimensional comparative space—France-England-America—informing most of Tocqueville's work. Within *Democracy in America*, Tocqueville artfully set Kentucky against Ohio, using the geographical proximity to underscore the sociopolitical distance, or Quebec against New Orleans, to cite but one more example among many. Schleifer lists a range of applications of this technique in discussing how Tocqueville "repeatedly clarified and deepened his thought by means of comparisons and distinctions" (1980, 279; see also Richter, 1970, 101). Thus the decision to travel the extreme distance, not merely in spatial terms, and write on America the Other must have been the result of a deliberate methodological choice.

Undoubtedly, these first two methodological reasons for choosing America had rhetorical counterparts as well. The absence of an entrenched literary competition enabled the young author to achieve an authoritative status more easily. The encounter with the fascinating Other ensured him of an attentive, curious audience. The very positioning across the Atlantic smoothed the delivery and reception of criticisms and suggestions for changes, a rhetorical strategy Tocqueville was conscious of at least vis-à-vis America: "Only strangers or experience may be able to bring certain truths to the American's attention" (DA, 256). Certainly, with regard to France, Tocqueville hoped his book would preempt the need for unhappy learning experiences. All these circumstances taken together were most propitious for the rapid achievement of glory, a goal young Tocqueville never denied harboring. Yet these rhetorical calculations, quite plausibly attributable to Tocqueville, do not contradict the methodological ones, but rather second them. Richter (1970, 88) quotes a revealing passage:

Should you explain the resemblances between the two countries, or write so as to enable the reader to find out? . . . In my work on America, I have almost always adopted the latter plan. Although I seldom mentioned France, I did not write a page without thinking of her, and placing her before me, as it were. . . . I believe that this perpetual silent reference to France was a principal cause of the book's success.

An examination of the third contribution of distance will dispel any doubts that methodological considerations were uppermost in Tocqueville's mind.

(3) The originality and boldness of Tocqueville's move, considering his personal background, have already been emphasized. However, his unusual care in disentangling himself from any partisan affiliation should be noted as well. In each volume of *Democracy in America*, the introduction ended with a warning in that regard. "This book is not precisely suited to anybody's taste," announced Tocqueville in 1835; "in writing it I did not intend to serve or to combat any party" (DA, 20). Five years later he wrote:

I hope that the impartiality for which my first book was credited will be found again in this work.

In the midst of the contradictory opinions that divide us, I have tried to divest myself for the moment of sympathies in favor of or instincts against each of them. If my readers find a single phrase calculated to flatter one of the great parties that have shaken our land or one of the petty factions which are now bringing on us confusion and paralysis, then let my readers raise their voices in protest against me. (DA, 418)

Those repeated promises and proud challenges were not mere rhetorical flourishes. A private letter to Henry Reeve, his translator, proves Tocqueville's sincerity and further clarifies his aim:

It has seemed to me that in the translation of the last book you have, without wishing it and following the instinct of your opinions, vividly colored what was contrary to democracy and rather softened what could harm aristocracy. I pray of you, therefore, to fight constantly against yourself on this point and to preserve the spirit of my book, which is one of the true impartiality in the theoretical judgment of the two societies, the old and new and also a sincere desire to see the new establish itself. (NC, 177–78)

Given Tocqueville's own (aristocratic) biography and inclinations, his admirable will to take distance in his analysis from arbitrary cultural values must be recognized. With this delineation of the contribution of Tocqueville's conscious distancing to a better articulation of the three junctures pointed out by Myrdal, the translation of Tocqueville's epistemological humility into practice has become clear. The methodology of distance ensures a systematic fleshing out of values and assumptions, making obvious their historical arbitrariness. For a theorist set against absolutist dictates, and striving to avoid subjectivism, submission to such a disciplined self-examination promotes a maximal heightening of awareness to cultural, political, and personal biases. Yet the effort of "distanciation," however scrupulously sustained, cannot on principle amount to a final, absolute cleansing: for all the reasons elaborated in Tocqueville's discussion of prejudice, one can never scrub out all the beliefs and assumptions embedded in one's conceptual world and attain divine objectivity. If only for that reason, the seeming discrepancy (which the meticulous reader might have detected) between some modern commentators' remarks on Tocqueville's partiality and his own mention of the considerable praise bestowed on his work for impartiality can be understood as a reflection of more than the arbitrariness of critics. Our distance from Tocqueville in itself suffices to bring out residues of normative embeddedness in mid-nineteenth-century European culture, which neither Tocqueville nor his contemporary critics had the necessary perspective to recognize.

Still, more than such unintentional normative residuals would be needed to forge the kind of powerful commitment earlier attributed to Tocqueville. While the contribution of methodological distance to the high degree of objectivity in Tocqueville's stand has been clarified, its role in maintaining normative commitment remains to be explained. Indeed, given the function of distance in forcing out implicit values and highlighting their cultural arbitrariness, it would seem to undermine—at least psychologically—the strength of any normative commitment. (Myrdal, 1969, 41, poses this dilemma in terms of remaining "practical" while being objective.) As analyzed so far, distance could appear to encourage an apathetic relativism. How does Tocqueville use it to maintain his powerful normative commitment?

Tocqueville's distance also involves a standing-apart in time. A carefully defined temporal perspective frames his study. Looking backward, America's privileged historical setting justifies its choice for Tocqueville's analysis. Close enough to its founding yet far enough along to gauge the results, "America is the only country in which we can watch the natural quiet growth of society and where it is possible to be exact about the influence of the point of departure on the future of a state" (DA, 32). From this ideal distance, one can secure the required knowledge, yet shed immediate personal interests and disregard short-term fluctuations. Temporal distance thus creates propitious conditions for safe judgment. This conclusion, however, would be reversed, should a symmetrical temporal perspective not be established toward the future. Simply passing a judgment as to present problems and opportunities, deducing immediate alternatives for action, would reactivate momentary interests and overemphasize temporary circumstances. Tocqueville accordingly creates a complementary forward-looking perspective: the time-horizon for his conclusions is consciously broadened. Indeed, on the heels of his promise to stay aloof from present partisan causes, he explains: "I have tried to see not differently but further than any party; while they are busy with tomorrow I have wished to consider the whole future" (DA, 20).

Distant considerations offer the surest means for highlighting the broadest, deepest normative concerns. Pitched at the highest level of abstraction, Tocqueville's ultimate judgments gain in intensity all they lose in immediacy and particularity. Such was the intent behind his emulation of the Divine perspective at the conclusion of Democracy in America: "It is natural to suppose that not the particular prosperity of the few, but the greater well-being of all, is most pleasing in the sight of the Creator and Preserver of men. What seems to me decay is thus in His eyes progress; what pains me is acceptable to Him. Equality may be less elevated, but it is more just, and in its justice lies its greatness and beauty" (DA, 704). Temporal distance, much more than an Almighty God (in which we cannot be confident Tocqueville indeed believed), brought out this ultimate normative judgment, Tocqueville's painful conversion from excellence to justice. It is thanks to that methodological strategy that "a strong case may therefore be made that Tocqueville's most essential concern was the moral condition of mankind" (Schleifer, 1980, 287). Enlarging one's temporal perspective provides an effective method for broadening as well as raising the stakes of the analysis: it thus brings out whatever normative commitment might be there, encouraging the theorist to take a stand.

Distance, however (to use a Heideggerian etymology), could also mean double-stance. Methodologically speaking, a corresponding strategy would involve assessing future alternatives from two normative perspectives. (Myrdal, 1969, 70, tentatively alludes to an ideal methodology relying on "several alternative sets of value premises.") While the analysis would thus be carried on from an explicitly normative standpoint, and even though the author's alternative description might be less than perfectly balanced, no absolute judgment would be rendered, leaving that task to the (consequently better informed) reader. Tocqueville regularly resorts to this strategy, in smaller and greater matters alike. An early discussion of administrative centralization delineates the advantages and disadvantages of such a policy, pitting gains in efficiency against gains in political freedom (and, as one can expect, not hiding Tocqueville's preference for the latter). *Democracy in America*'s last pages, as was already noted, are preoccupied with this problem of value trade-off as well. Aristocracy and democracy qua normative systems are contrasted (DA,

704–5), with Tocqueville drawing two intriguing conclusions. Applying a set of standards derived from one to the other is meaningless—these systems are incommensurable (DA, 705); and, given the progress of democracy, the sole actual tradeoff lies between equality and liberty. Tocqueville's rhetorical formulation takes a more tendentious form, succinctly summarized in this draft for the second volume: "Two questions to resolve. Despotism with equality. Liberty with equality. The whole question of the future rests there" (Schleifer, 1980, 187). Still, as any reader of *Democracy in America* knows, and indeed anyone reflecting on the present political situation realizes, the problem remains one of balancing the claims of two primary values: liberty and equality.

Abstracting from this illustration, however important in its own right, we can learn a clear methodological lesson. As a methodological strategy, the delineation of value trade-offs by itself fulfills the two requirements of Tocqueville's normative stand: it necessarily involves explicit normative evaluation, while refraining from subjective conclusions. This dual character endows it with particular worth, and justifies the further attempts at a more abstract theoretical formulation, undertaken in the next chapter.

Taken together, both extended time-horizons and compared value trade-offs contribute to the second part of Tocqueville's stand. They each help sustain an explicitly normatively informed analysis. A consciously achieved distance thus enables Tocqueville to maintain simultaneously a powerful normative commitment and a cautious avoidance of subjectivism. With this conclusion, we are ready to summarize the findings of our case study.

Tocqueville's normative stand, the relation between his analysis and the values he espouses, presents an unconventional blend of explicit normative orientation and determined striving toward objectivity, in a spirit of resolute antiabsolutism. To translate this (at least psychologically) tense combination into practice, Tocqueville resorts to what was termed here a

methodology of distance. A conscious distancing from his subject matter, from his intellectual and political milieu, and a
comparative strategy designed to force out implicit assumptions ensured a high degree of objectivity and epistemological
humility. A strategy of delineating value trade-offs, helping as
well to shun absolute conclusions, dictated the adoption of
a normative perspective, a commitment secured by enlarging
the time-horizon to broaden and heighten the stakes and encourage the taking of a stand. Are these strategies peculiar to
Democracy in America? Can this characterization of Tocqueville's normative stand apply to his work as a whole? These
questions are addressed in the next chapter.

CHAPTER 7

Normative Stand, in Tocqueville
and in Social Theory

The argument of the preceding case study must now be generalized, on two ascending levels: Is the normative stand exhibited in *Democracy in America* a recurrent, intrinsic element of Tocqueville's method? Could it justifiably be viewed as an essential component of social theory? Given the novelty of the definition of Tocqueville's normative stand, my attempt to answer these two queries will find little to affirm or deny in the comments of earlier exegetes and the dictates of previous methodologists. Still, whenever other commentators either corroborate or challenge some step in my argument their claims will be addressed. Thus, for example, Sainte-Beuve's observation that "no one has ever scrutinized his own thoughts more conscientiously than Tocqueville, no one has ever exposed them more sincerely" (1860, 326) clearly testifies to one aspect—the relentless uncovering of implicit assumptions—of the complex blend constituting Tocqueville's methodology of distance. Before we verify the pervasiveness of this methodology in Tocqueville's work, a short recapitulation of key elements is in order.

Normative Stands Generally

The preceding chapter presented a convenient characterization of two extreme normative stands: the "classical" ethical commitment and the "modern" objective detachment. Both stands, it was emphasized, were designed to achieve absolute knowledge and attain certainty. Against this shorthand description of an endless debate on the proper attitude toward the normative in social theory, Tocqueville's stand emerged as a complex, indeed puzzling synthesis: normative commitment coupled with a striving toward objectivity, in a spirit of resolute antiabsolutism. The coexistence of these usually conflicting orientations was documented in the case of *Democracy in America*, with the promise of picking up in due time some crucial unresolved issues, such as Tocqueville's attitude toward religion. In particular, one previous interpretation of Tocqueville's normative approach was deemed worthy of subsequent discussion. Marvin Zetterbaum appeared to have reached, earlier on, a conclusion similar to mine: "[Tocqueville's] achievement was to have combined [this] deep concern with a perfectly balanced sense of scientific objectivity" (1967, 17). Zetterbaum further qualified this singular mix of classical and modern stands by noting Tocqueville's rejection of the overly ambitious "study of Man" in favor of a contextual inquiry of particular social conditions (1972, 657). However, Zetterbaum ultimately slighted the extent of Tocqueville's originality, noting that, after all, "the status of social condition as the fundamental cause in his work is ultimately ambiguous" (1967, 138). Tocqueville, according to Zetterbaum, ended up proclaiming "solutions of political art" (1972, 669) that "probably would not have struck even a classical political philosopher as unique" (1967, 137). In sum, for Zetterbaum "it is strange that [Tocqueville] felt compelled to call for a new science of politics" (1967, 137).

In contrast my case study, dedicated to the identification of the novelty of Tocqueville's normative stand, uncovered as the key to its translation into practice a "methodology of distance": a conscious distancing from the subject matter, as well as one's intellectual and political milieu, and a comparative approach aimed at forcing out implicit assumptions secured both objectivity and epistemological humility. An enlargement of the time-horizon to distance, yet broaden and heighten the stakes, and a strategy of delineating value trade-offs of political alternatives encouraged normative commitment and ruled out absolute conclusions. Does this methodology of distance operate in Tocqueville's other works?

Normative Stand in Tocqueville

A recent exegete harshly condemns Tocqueville for the alleged aristocratic complacency with which he anchors his self and his work, signing "Alexis de Tocqueville, from Tocqueville" (Hertz, 1985, 179). In truth the *Recollections* offer ample evidence of Tocqueville's acute awareness of his social and cultural milieu praised by Sainte-Beuve: "My origin and the world in which I had been brought up gave me great advantages here, which the others did not have" (R, 217; see also DA, 259). Despite the official demise of the aristocracy, it remained a powerful, secret "sort of freemasonry." Scrutinizing his own conscience Tocqueville admits, in a footnote, that "The link that exists between all its members is invisible, but it is so close that I have found myself a hundred times more at ease dealing about some matter with aristocrats whose interests and opinions were entirely different from mine, than with the bourgeois whose ideas I shared and whose interests were similar to my own" (R, 217n4).

To this relentless examination of one's prejudices corresponds a perpetual questioning of one's society's dictates. An "ancient tradition" of French diplomacy would have it that a fragmented Germany serves France's interest best. Yet, should one be willing to enlarge the time-horizon of political decisions, the slow rise of Russia clearly would prompt a repudiation of such accepted wisdom: "The state of the world is new: we must change our old maxims" (R, 247), warns the ex-foreign minister. By a similar procedure the theorist, approaching the already overanalyzed and politically laden sub-

ject of the 1789 revolution, drastically distances himself from
all acquired wisdom:

> When I have some subject to deal with, I find it almost impossible to read
> any of the books that have been written on the same matter. Contact with
> the ideas of others agitates and troubles me so much that my reading
> of those works becomes painful. I abstain then as much as I can from
> learning how their authors have interpreted the facts that interest me
> and what are their judgments and the various ideas suggested to them by
> these facts. (Quoted in Herr, 1962, 66)

Beyond these examples, culled almost at random, the *Recollections'* opening provides the best testimony for Tocqueville's conscious methodology of distance. Positioned "out of
the stream of public life" (R, 3), Tocqueville can turn to study
"events of the recent past" (R, 3)—that is, those not so close as
to blur his perspective (R, 4). To capture "the uncertain physiognomy" of his time Tocqueville needs both personal distance,
afforded by the forced transition to private life, and temporal
distance, which restores intelligibility to the chaotic events of
1848 (on which see the long paragraph joining R, 4–5).
    Any doubts as to the methodical nature of this careful po-
sitioning are dispelled when one sees the procedure repeated,
with greater emphasis and elaboration, in the opening pages of
The Old Regime and the French Revolution. Tocqueville de-
cides to study the revolution at the perfect moment for understanding it:

> I believe that the time has come when these questions can be answered;
> that today we are in a position to see this memorable event in its true
> perspective and pass judgment on it. For we now are far enough from
> the Revolution to be relatively unaffected by the frenzied enthusiasm of
> those who saw it through; yet near enough to be able to enter into the
> feelings of its promoters and to see what they were aiming at. Soon it
> will be difficult to do this; since when great revolutions are successful
> their causes cease to exist, and the very fact of their success has made
> them incomprehensible. (AR, 4–5; see also 134)

An earlier letter to Mme. de Circourt expresses the same
consciousness of the importance of distance, confirming that

Tocqueville's published words were not merely a late embellishment added to the introductory chapter of a completed study (OC, 85; a similar, until recently unpublished letter is quoted by Jardin, 1984, 386). Moreover, as the foremost student of *The Old Regime and the French Revolution*, Richard Herr, repeatedly noted (1962, 19, 31), Tocqueville also aimed to exploit the temporal distance between the Old Regime and his days in the opposite direction: often his analysis reads like a pamphlet for political change. A careful reader, and certainly Tocqueville's contemporaries, can easily detect heavy hints at the decay of French public spirit—"a slave mentality in the very exercise of its freedom" (AR, 137)—and even some shocking, loaded turns of phrases from the pen of a cautious conservative: "revolution, that last resort of an indignant nation" (AR, 101).

Tocqueville's normative commitment is just as clear as his attempt to achieve an objective perspective. The foreword is most explicit in this regard: "I hope and believe that I have written the present book without any *parti pris*, though it would be futile to deny that my own feelings were engaged. What Frenchman can write about his country and think about the age in which he lives in a spirit of complete detachment? Thus I confess that when studying our old social system under its infinitely various aspects I have never quite lost sight of present-day France" (AR, xi–xii). If novelists have but one story to tell, and political theorists one creed to defend, then Tocqueville, once more, is promoting the pure, unadulterated love of freedom (AR, 168–69, 210).

That overriding concern explains some of Tocqueville's harsh judgments of his contemporaries or his eighteenth-century aristocratic ancestors, which Arthur Stinchcombe simply ascribed to "conservative despair" (1978, 2), proposing in consequence "that we ignore de Tocqueville's historical method whenever its purpose is to present a praiseworthy feudal regime to contrast with the bad Old Regime" (1978, 44). Stinchcombe, evidently, demands an outright condemnation of any hierarchical system, and a comforting narrative of linear moral and political progress. Tocqueville, however, is again engaged in the thorough balancing of value trade-offs. Even forms of servitude must be distinguished: a natural, filial and religious love for King is preferable to a fearful subservience to illegitimate or dubious authority (AR, 119). Tocqueville's ancestors "still could call their souls their own," while his contemporaries betray "a servile mind" (AR, 119). Concerted praise for the aristocracy is not mere aristocratic bias, as Stinchcombe would have it (1978, 42), but rather the result of a normatively minded sociological analysis: "When a class has taken the lead in public affairs for centuries, it develops as a result of this long, unchallenged habit of pre-eminence a certain proper pride and confidence in its strength, leading it to be the point of maximum resistance in the social organism. And it not only has itself the manly virtues; by dint of its example it quickens them in other classes" (AR, 111). In fact, Tocqueville also compares favorably the common citizen of eighteenth-century France to his contemporaries. His delineation of the value trade-offs is worth citing at length:

Eighteenth-Century man had little of that craving for material well-being which leads the way to servitude. A craving which, while morally debilitating, can be singularly tenacious and insidious, it often operates in close association with such private virtues as family love, a sense of decorum, respect for religion, and even a lukewarm but punctilious observance of the rites of the established Church. While promoting moral rectitude, it rules out heroism and excels in making people well behaved but mean-spirited as citizens. (AR, 118)

The reader can further convince herself of the pervasiveness of this double-stand approach throughout Tocqueville's work by consulting a similar analysis of equality in the United States and France (DA, 259–61).

Finally, Tocqueville's use of comparative methods to uncover and highlight political and cultural assumptions generally is evident throughout *The Old Regime and the French Revolution*. Certainly, to understand French politics, one needs to study the international context and examine France's neighbors (AR, 19). More strikingly still, to demonstrate the long-standing—yet rarely perceived—French tradition of overcentralization, Tocqueville offers an original comparison of Canada and the United States: "The physiognomy of governments can be best detected in their colonies, for there their features are magnified, and rendered more conspicuous" (AR, 253). Broad comparative strokes of this kind can lead to bold conclusions. Thus the French Revolution, when one considers its penchant for abstractions, its disregard for particularities of times and places, in short its universalizing absolutism, must be deemed a religious revolution (AR, 12). Let it be clear, however, that this surprising conclusion is meant as an accusation: it is time to address more specifically Tocqueville's attitude toward religion and, by extension, all claims to absolute truth.

No one, having studied Tocqueville's complete works, especially the numerous letters lamenting the inability to believe (see Jardin, 1984, 484), could harbor any doubts concerning Tocqueville's personal attitude to religion. His most recent and thorough biographer, André Jardin, rightly concludes that Tocqueville was not a believer (1984, 499). In fact, considering the overwhelming evidence backing this conclusion, one wonders how the issue of Tocqueville's personal faith ever became controversial. At the most immediate level the answer lies with Mary Mottley, Tocqueville's wife, a devoted convert to Catholicism.

Having enjoyed little success in influencing her husband, Mary resolved at least to shape his image for posterity. She thus threatened to take Falloux to court should he publish Tocqueville's revealing letter to Mme. Swetchine (Jardin, 1984, 54), and pressured Beaumont to modify his account of Tocqueville's last days (Jardin, 1984, 500). The letter to Swetchine, inexplicably absent from Boesche's recent compilation of the *Selected Letters* (1985), is an invaluable document for anyone interested in Tocqueville's intellectual and religious development. It poignantly recounts the eruption of "universal doubt"

into Tocqueville's soul, at sixteen, and particularly his irrevocable loss of religious faith (see Jardin, 1984, 62–63). While
the black depression brought about by this crisis subsided,
Tocqueville never recovered his faith, and indeed came to believe one is either blessed with it at birth or forever distant
(see Jardin, 1984, 428). Suspicious accounts of his deathbed
conversion only testify to the absence of faith throughout his
life. The unconvincing evidence of Beaumont's published testimony, especially given his contradictory statement to Senior,
and the resolute silence of Tocqueville's close friends and com-
panions on his last days, Kergolay and Corcelle, once more
betray Mary Mottley's distorting influence (see Jardin, 1984,
500–504).

Yet a subtler reason explains the widespread acceptance,
among Tocqueville scholars, of the image carefully shaped
by his wife: Tocqueville, after all, had much use for religion
politically. However, he never welcomed the absolutism inherent in all theologies, or the fanatical sectarianism of the
churches, foremost among them the Catholic church (see DA,
369). The intolerance of absolutism seemed to him socially
dangerous and intellectually arrogant (SL, 50). More particularly, he judged the ideal of *imitatio cristi* "supremely im-
moral": those living by such dictates "cannot fail to lose everything that constitutes public virtues" (SL, 357). Abandoning
"the despair of seeking the truth" and welcoming the church's
authority spells the sacrifice of reason (SL, 51). Nevertheless, these views had to be kept private—*in petto* (SL, 51)—
for political reasons. Tocqueville explains his noble lie: "Can
deism ever be suitable for all classes of a people? Especially for
those who have the most need to have the bridle of religion?
That is what I cannot convince myself of" (SL, 52).

Thus, at least on the topic of religion and its role in society Tocqueville rejected absolute answers: "The only absolute truth that I see in this matter is that there is no absolute
truth" (SL, 193). Was that rejection of metanarratives, to use
a currently fashionable phrase, extended to other realms as

well? Writing to his intimate friend, Charles Stoffels, Tocqueville describes the quest for certainty as "yet another chimera of youth" (SL, 63). The profound metaphysical crisis of his adolescence indeed reached beyond the realm of faith. At its conclusion Tocqueville became convinced "that the search for absolute, *demonstrable* truth, like the quest for perfect happiness, was an effort directed toward the impossible.... Concerning the immense majority of points that it is important for us to know, we have only probabilities, almosts" (SL, 64). This quasi post-modern stand, however, did not translate into disenchanted nihilism. While no one can deny the contingency of sociopolitical institutions, wrote Tocqueville, "the duty of honest people is not any the less to defend the only one they understand, and even to be killed for it, while waiting to be shown a better" (SL, 251).

What, then, would be the duty of the honest theorist? Handling the fabric of facts must be combined with judging them: objectivity, somehow, must be accompanied by normative commitment. Tocqueville's profound awareness of the nature and difficulties of his stand is beautifully expressed in a letter to Kergolay concerning the writing of *The Old Regime and the French Revolution*:

> But the difficulties are immense. The one that most troubles my mind comes from the mixture of history properly so called with historical philosophy. I still do not see how to mix these two things (and yet, they must be mixed, for one could say that the first is the canvas and the second the color, and that it is necessary to have both at the same time in order to do the picture). I fear that the one is harmful to the other.... (SL, 256)

Furthermore, Tocqueville carefully adumbrates the nature of his normative evaluations. One must shun prejudices and short-run judgments of "constitutions, laws, dynasties, classes": solely at issue are their long-range moral and political effects (SL, 257). "I have no traditions, I have no party, I have no *cause*, if it is not that of liberty and human dignity" (SL, 257). Yet Tocqueville's readers are not left without a clear lesson, without any suggestions whatsoever (SL, 293). Rather, Tocqueville sets "their minds on the road leading to truths"— a most significant plural—and makes them "find these truths for themselves" (SL, 294). Clearly, Tocqueville is aware of the importance of an extended time-horizon and a comparison of value trade-offs as strategies to develop objective yet nonabsolutist normative conclusions—the asymptotic goal that defines his stand.

The Place of Normative Stand

To make a case for the necessity of normative import would smack of a positivism rejected earlier, by the very implication that somehow the normative could be cleansed out of one's analysis and facts and values could be radically disengaged. "A disinterested social science has never existed and, for logical reasons, can never exist" wrote Myrdal (1969, 55). More specifically, Cannon finds objectivity in history a sham ideal, unrealizable and dangerous: nothing more misleading than a historian claiming (and possibly believing in) objectivity. Hence the praise of Tocqueville's self-consciousness, his expressed determination to write "without prejudice but not without passion" (Cannon, 1980, 74). The phrase perfectly captures the distinction between covert, petty biases of the day, which can only impoverish the analysis, and open, principled longstanding commitments that lend it unusual strength.

Indeed Chapters 2 and 5 both concluded with a call for a normative moment to complete the task of social theory. Hermeneutics as well as formal modeling were seen to be faced with a loose relativism, an abdication of judgment among personal ends as well as forms of life, while the instinctive irrationalism of the interpretive bow to the authority of tradition echoed the artificial rationalism of the rational actor approach toward individual preference formation. In both cases the analysis unwittingly absorbed accepted value judgments without openly taking a stand, never for a moment escaping the ruling ideology without, however, accepting responsibility. The need for a "responsible ideology" (Connolly, 1967, 152), an explicit normative stand, thus was made clear.

The Dangers of Distance

Having introduced, in the last chapter, Tocqueville's singularly developed methodology of distance, and having observed —there as well as in the first part of this chapter—its usefulness in defining a normative stand, I take one last important step before recommending it to social theorists generally. Like every other method, distancing can be abused or misused and can lead to undesirable results. While Tocqueville seems to have been successful in shying away from absolutism while maintaining a passionate, explicit normative commitment, neither aspect of this achievement should be considered merely a given consequence of the methodology of distance. Its potential dangers are best discussed under two separate headings: the epistemological and the psychological.

Pierre Bourdieu has explored thoroughly the epistemological pitfalls of intellectual distance. Ironically observing that, in many cases, what masquerades as a methodological choice is nothing but the inevitable condition of the ethnologist, Bourdieu wishes to reconsider the subsequent extolling of the virtues unwittingly achieved by this imposed outsider status (1972, 159). To him the perspective taken on practice, its likely objectification as a system of codes and rules, are but a step away from essentialism—witness Chomsky's "linguistic competence" and later Habermas's "universal pragmatics." In light of such overambitious reconceptualizations, Tocqueville's cautious avoidance of absolute, universal conclusions appears to be a singular achievement, the fruit of personal determinations much more than of the methodology adopted. What Bourdieu suspects as inherent in the methodology of distance, and fears, is the mirror problem of the one explored in Chapter 5 under the heading of "The Danger of Subjectivism": too radical a rupture with practice, too sharp a break with the familiarity of the participant must distort understanding and consequently hinder the possibility of being understood.

The psychological problem connected with the methodology of distance, as my terminology is designed to suggest, is not a logical, necessary result of the normative distance assumed by the theorist. Yet the moral/political paralysis somehow triggered by the "disenchantment" of modernity, to use a term proposed by one who felt it deeply, is a well-recognized if not fully understood phenomenon. The distance from one's *Sittlichkeit* achieved through a comparative historical approach, or the mere recognition of inevitable value trade-offs in the transition between forms of life, or simply the acknowledgement of contingency in the development of allegedly "natural" and "necessary" norms of belief and practice accompanying critical theoretical reflection—all display a tendency to undermine normative commitment of any kind. Vincent Descombes succinctly describes the predicament in the specific case of religious faith, and the links to Tocqueville's personal life and public work are obvious. "This same religion, which in an age of faith was holy, became somewhat tainted after the age of criticism, when the Romantics sought to restore it, out of a nostalgia for childhood, as did the political thinkers, so that the people might have morality, and the religious thinkers themselves to avoid despair" (1980, 182). Generalizing the dilemma, can we keep separate the "two parallel planes in our mind," as Koestler (1984, 133) counsels, "the plane of detached contemplation under the sign of infinity, and the plane of action in the name of certain ethical imperatives," once they have come to coexist in tension with one another? Can one renounce absolutism, accept a "world well-lost" (Rorty, 1972) to our best efforts at representing it truthfully, and still passionately care? Can the best not lack conviction?

Michael Walzer's recent study of social criticism (1987, 50–51) targeted the concept of distance, centering precisely on the two dangers described above. In Walzer's terms, these are the intellectual and emotional by-products of "radical detachment" (1987, 77). The wrenching loose from "parochial interests and loyalties" (1987, 5) too often results in a dangerous estrangement from membership in one's moral and intellectual community, exemplified by Lenin's abstract imposition of an alien blueprint on rural and religious Russia (Walzer, 1987, 63). Walzer's counterideal is the "connected critic," "one of us" who perhaps has had the advantage of traveling (1987, 39), a slim concession to the necessity of a comparative perspective. After all, even the original *theōros* was chosen for his ability, acquired through the experience of local practices *and* the distance created by traveling, of re-presenting his own society to its members from a critical perspective.

Thus, the terms of the debate have been set. Taking into consideration the inspiring example of Tocqueville's systematic distancing, and the thought-provoking criticisms summed up by Walzer, an argument for the role of the methodology of distance in social theory must be developed. We now turn to answer the second question posed at the outset of this chapter: Do the potential contributions and detractions of the methodology of distance justify viewing it as an essential component of social theory?

Normative Stand in Social Theory

The conception of social theory emerging from this study so far takes for granted the inevitability of normative implications in any social analysis, and further welcomes the explicit adoption of a normative stand as a necessary corrective to what is lacking in both formal modeling and hermeneutic inquiries. Consequently the issue in this section cannot simply be the pros and cons of carrying normative implications, or even the desirability of a consciously elaborated normative stand. Rather, in line with the initial strategy of learning from actual practice, the task here will be to examine the characteristics of one specific methodology for incorporating the normative in social theory, the methodology of distance.

This examination bears a structural resemblance to those carried out at the conclusions of Chapters 3 and 5, such as the division into two subsections. The subject matter, though, calls for a slightly different treatment, following the distinction clarified in the preceding section. The question of theoretical fruitfulness, earlier subsumed under the heading of "truth-value," will here be addressed as the epistemology of distance. The questions of normative implications, the "justice-value" of the methodology, makes sense only as an examination of the psychology of distance: the focus shifts from a concern with the normative import of the theory to a concern with the normative commitment of the theorist. While the theory, informed by the methodology of distance, would include an explicit normative stand by definition, we have seen how the resolve of the theorist to take a stand can appear problematic. The question then is: Does the methodology of distance dilute or strengthen the capacity of the theorist to take a stand?

Having answered this question, the section will conclude with a brief summary of this chapter's findings, clearing the way for the last chapter's attempt to reconstruct Tocqueville's method as a coherent whole, and offer this synthesis as a model for social theory.

The Epistemology of Distance

Ce point indivisible que la perspective assigne dans l'art de la peinture, qui donc dans la vérité et la morale l'assignera?   —PASCAL

Long before the discovery of the perspective in pictorial representation, the notion of distance as a requirement for conceptual clarity in social and political matters was well established. Leaving behind the institution of the *theōros*, at least since Plato's symbolic and practical positioning of his Academy outside the city walls, distance has been a crucial, persistent element in lasting works of social theory. As Sheldon Wolin's discussion of the issue makes clear, the theorist's detachment can be measured along two dimensions, "establishing not only space between politics and the theorist but a different order of time for putting the present and the emerging future into 'perspective'" (1980, 198–99). Unsurprisingly, Wolin finds "the perfect account of the theorist's quest for distance" in Tocqueville, specifically in the metaphorical description in *Democracy in America* of Tocqueville's retreat from the city and ascent to the top of the neighboring mountain. Beyond such metaphors, however, at issue remains the epistemological import of temporal and spatial, historical and anthropological distance.

The work of Louis Dumont offers a systematic explanation, and exploitation, of the epistemological benefits of distance, and in the process refutes the charges brought against it by Bourdieu. Cultural comparison in the human sciences, writes Dumont, is the counterpart of the essential external fulcrum in the physical sciences (1977, 11); one cannot move a mass from within, or understand the familiar without witnessing the strange. Conceived in this manner, distance—be it across time or space—is not simply the opportunistically glorified predicament of historical or anthropological research, but rather the opportunity to generate comparisons, hence discover one's true particularity. Acquiring the first component of the normative stand advocated here, following Tocqueville, is made easy by this use of distance: the rejection of metanarratives derives its motivation from the recovery of the conventional and the contingent at the heart of our norms and institutions, which is made possible by the comparative approach. While Bourdieu worries about essentialism and reification in the study of the other, Dumont shows the undoing of these attitudes in the understanding of the self.

Thus Dumont's immersion in the Indian social system becomes the key to a hard-won differentiation between the individual as an "empirical subject of speech, thought and will" and as an "independent, autonomous moral being" (1970b, 135). Disentangling the empirical contrast from the peculiar

ideological construct of modern, liberal industrial society—
routinely taken, within it, as a universal fact—was made possible solely by the theorist's distanciation.

Once more, it should be noted, Dumont's model and inspiration with regard to this methodology is Tocqueville. Tocqueville's achievements in comparing the new, emerging egali-
tarian mentality with the old, familiar hierarchical mentality
prompted Dumont to attempt, a century of democracy later,
the reverse conceptual adventure (1970a, 16–17). Dumont's
remarkable comparative history and anthropology is modeled
after Tocqueville's concrete study of the implication of the
shift of values generated by the advent of liberal democracy
(1970a, 15–16), an application of the methodology of distance described here as the examination of value trade-offs
(see Chapter 6 above).

This aspect of the methodology, though, naturally leads us
to the second question to be examined, and the second, complementing component of the normative stand hereby advocated. The double normative stance, "distance" embodied in
the strategy of delineating value trade-offs, logically enables
the theorist to commit herself normatively while eschewing
absolute answers. As Hayden White notes, Tocqueville's aim
was "to ground living men in a situation of choice, to enliven
them to the possibilities of choosing, and to inform them of the
difficulties attending any choice they might make" (1973, 205).
Yet, beyond logical possibilities, can one abandon all pretensions to absolute answers and retain a passionate normative
commitment?

The Psychology of Distance

Il faut que je fasse comme les peintres, et que je m'éloigne, mais non pas de
trop, de combien? Devinez. —PASCAL

Assuming the epistemological benefits of distance justify an
adoption of the methodology, we must ask the question, as
Pascal well saw, of how far one should go. Is there a model
to be followed, a defined point beyond which healthy impar-

tiality turns into pathological indifference? Richard Brown, in his search for an objective interpretive sociological method (1977), identifies both a specific model and a general phenomenological description of the proper use of distance. "Tocqueville was 'distanced' not only in his general theoretical stance; he also had the built-in psychic distance of an outsider. He was an aristocrat in an age of egalitarianism, yet he was marginal to the aristocracy itself. He was at once a scholar and a man of practical affairs. Most important, he was a Frenchman in a foreign land" (1977, 55). Tocqueville's achievements can in part be ascribed to this fortunate social and political positioning, and in turn they illustrate the benefits of the methodology of distance. Yet, while Brown's description wonderfully corroborates the analysis of the previous chapter, it remains of little help to the would be theorist: one would be hard pressed to duplicate a "built-in" distance similar to the one with which Tocqueville was naturally endowed. To that effect Brown points to a phenomenological description of the "optimal perspective for apprehending social reality," centered around a "standing apart from conventional categories" (1977, 52, 51)—Simmel's classic essay on "The Stranger" (1971).

Precisely the same reference, however, is identified by Walzer as the typical example of a confusion of marginality and objectivity (1987, 37). Looking as well to determine "how much distance critical distance is" (1987, 36), Walzer sketches a simplified dichotomy opposing, as early models of social critics, a successful to an unsuccessful prophet—Amos to Jonah (1987, 77). Coming from outside to the pagan city of Nineveh, Jonah has little affective common ground with its inhabitants, and precious few shared values from which to build a shared normative discourse. Amos, on the contrary, preaches to his countrymen in a language they understand, literally and figuratively. The voice of the tradition, expressed through him, lends him an undeniable authority, even though his audience has turned away from the divinely ordained ways.

Despite Walzer's reverence for the biblical tradition, his interpretation in this case flies in the face of conventional exegesis, Jewish and Christian alike. The powerful impact of Jonah, the outsider, on the city of Nineveh, is often compared favorably in the New Testament to the failure of Jesus himself and his disciples in their own land (e.g. Matthew, 13:41). In the words of Matthew, paraphrasing Jesus, that failure is generalized into a universal rule: "A prophet is not without honor, save in his own country, and in his own house" (Matthew, 13:57). Talmudic wisdom as well testifies that no prophet achieves recognition in his own city (indeed the phrase has become a casually used proverb in modern Hebrew). Moreover the substantive basis for Walzer's distinction, the alleged lack of common normative ground, slights the universalist strain in Judaism, the belief in a universally binding core of ethical precepts known as the Noachic Laws.

Biblical hermeneutics aside, it would seem that Walzer's reading of Simmel's portrait erases all the nuances characterizing the stranger's position. To see in him merely a detached dispassionate outsider lacking all commitment is to miss the complexities of Simmel's analysis, which Brown sums up under the by now familiar label of di-stance, a dual stance (1977, 52). Simmel himself writes of "a distinct structure composed of remoteness and nearness, indifference and involvement" (1971, 145). The stranger's objectivity "is by no means nonparticipation," "mere detachment": rather, this particular social location strengthens normative commitment of a particular kind. "It is rather a positive and definite kind of participation," characterized by the unique freedom of one not bound to "particular constituents and partisan dispositions of the group," not restrained "by ties which could prejudice his perception, his understanding, and his assessment of data" (Simmel, 1971, 145, 146). Simmel's choice of words strikingly echoes Tocqueville's self-description, particularly in the common emphasis on the shedding of petty prejudices and the disregard for short-run interests, advantageously replaced by "standards that are more general and more objective" (1971, 146). To these, indeed, his commitment is unwavering, as Tocqueville's lifelong dedication to individual freedom exemplifies. Commitment to fundamental principles emerges purified and strengthened thanks to the methodology of distance. In sum, I contend that a close rereading of Simmel's piece would minimize the distance between Brown's sociologist as "stranger" and Walzer's "connected critic."

One advantage, however, can be ascribed to Walzer's model. Intuitively—for the subject remains undeveloped in his monograph—Walzer chose to focus on the paradigm of long-range thinking, the prophet. Leaving aside divine revelations and apocalyptic visions, the temporal distancing characterizing prophetic warnings immediately lifts their social criticisms above the petty disputes of the day. Certainly, it is worth repeating, Tocqueville was no prophet. This whole study is predicated on a belief in the superiority of his methodology rather than in the good fortune of his alleged knack for inspired guesses. The point here, rather, is Tocqueville's specific emphasis on his determination to see further, to address long-range developments. Such a conscious broadening of the time-horizon of the analysis immediately and effortlessly disentangles one from parochial and personal ties and influences that perforce loom large in short-range political commentaries. This effect can be formally demonstrated, and indeed has been in the paradigm case of creating a society, entering the social contract. Classical political philosophers (e.g. Rousseau) as well as contemporary game theorists (e.g. Taylor, 1976) agree on the crucial import of "vision" or "high discount rate for immediate payoffs" in the effort to capture, socially and politically speaking, the two birds in the bush (see Hadari, 1986). What is more, within an enlarged time-horizon, the theorist's commitment to a set of values can be affirmed without the dogmatic accompaniment of specific dictates for immediate action: antiabsolutism and passionate commitment find ample room for accommodation in this broadened theoretical space.

It is tempting to speculate that, in social theory as well as chess, the capacity to see further moves ahead distinguishes grand masters from amateurs. Once more, in any case, distance strengthens the possibility of defining a normative stand.

Thus the case for distance has been made. Its epistemological benefits are clear, and not only does it not logically preclude normative commitment, it eases it by shedding short-term concerns, hence purifying the theorist's inner core of fundamental values bearing long-range implications. The methodology of distance seems particularly suited for developing and strengthening the kind of normative stand advocated here, following Tocqueville's example: a firm rejection of absolutism coupled with an explicit normative commitment.

Time thus has come for taking some distance from this necessarily fragmented study, to gain some perspective on Tocqueville's three-tiered method as one coherent whole. This will be the task of the next, concluding chapter, which will end on a bid for this method as a proven way to yield still better social theory.

CHAPTER 8

Conclusion

The reconstruction of Tocqueville's method proceeded from the ground up, and aimed to recover three key elements: formal models, hermeneutics, and normative stand. The point that must now be emphasized is Tocqueville's method as a whole—the topic of the book though of none of its chapters. The three methodological moments examined in isolation in the three parts do not appear in such disconnected form in Tocqueville's text. Under no circumstances do they reflect some fixed chronology in the logic of discovery. My presentation follows no formulaic sequence, its order being determined by a rhetorical ordering of the texts themselves, as I made clear in the introduction. The embeddedness of the formal models in a wealth of hermeneutic insights guarantees the historical perspective, so sorely missing in most "rational actor" analyses; it ensures the use of an appropriate concept of rationality. The normative stand is not added at the end of the writing, the way one saves a few cloves of garlic to add character to a steaming casserole: it informs the quest and its findings, the questions posed and the answers—preferably new questions—reached. The painstaking task of detecting and lifting out each of these three elements, even in the passages of Tocqueville's work especially preselected to strengthen my case, amply demonstrates their interdependence and unity.

However, perhaps this cautious preselection itself, though commonly allowed an author, will appear suspect to some. Let me then offer a brief example of Tocqueville at work, spontaneously integrating the three parts of his overall methodology artificially separated in this study. No need for careful preselection in this case. Open the first volume of Tocqueville's first book, and reach for his first sociotheoretical analysis (DA, 51, past introductory delineations of the geographical and historical parameters of the American democratic experiment), and a superb example of his method at work offers itself to you. The topic seems banal enough, indeed hardly promising in terms of subtle analysis and far-reaching insights: the law of inheritance. Tocqueville's presentation immediately suggests more. He sees that law laying "hands on each generation before it is born," hence endowing man "with almost supernatural power over the future" (DA, 51).

Viewed as a political-economic mechanism, it either "assembles, concentrates, piles up property" or "divides, shares, and spreads property and power" (DA, 52). With all crucial parameters defined, one could model the "physical effect of the law" (DA, 52). In its latter, democratic version, property changes not only hands, but nature, as its division into smaller fractions diminishes its size. However, should the average fertility rate be two children (Tocqueville lacks that statistic for the United States, but notices it is closer to three in France), on average the individual child should not end up poorer than each parent was.

Important as this abstract model is—find the appropriate statistics, and you can apply it anywhere the law takes effect —it entirely misses a crucial sentimental element lost in those transactions. The law of inheritance, any student of mores will attest, "also affects the very soul of the landowner" (DA, 52). Primogeniture binds land and family feeling indissolubly, perpetuating "name, origin, glory, power, and virtue," linking past to future in a reassuring, unquestionable way (DA, 52). The new law thus signifies the irrevocable break between land preservation and family feeling, ultimately erasing it even should the family's economic status be sustained by other means (DA, 53). Indeed, the temptation to sell real estate is great, given the higher interest available through other investments in this age of industrial revolution. These simple, allegedly neutral economic formulas, promising immediate satisfaction to the passions of the moment, prompt a reevaluation of all values: thus do memory and pride bow to interest and liquidity.

Tocqueville, it is worth mentioning, makes one mistake in this analysis, judging it unlikely that anybody—besides risk-averse traditionalists and the poor, faithful to their love of the land (DA, 54n3)—will fight the current and consolidate vast properties (DA, 53): smaller plots yield better revenues. "Chance," in its most familiar guise of radical technological innovations, made the prophecy of massive agribusiness inaccessible.

Finally, this dialectic of things affecting persons, who in turn affect things in a spiral of growing complexity (DA, 53), thus imposing a blend of formal models and hermeneutic queries, bears normative consequences. Often, writes our cynical Frenchman, "family feeling" is but "personal selfishness" writ large, a patriarch's quest for illusory immortality. Stripped of its main tangible center, the magnet, the anchor of landed property, "the family is felt to be a vague, indeterminate" conception, hence "personal selfishness turns again to its real inclinations" (DA, 53). "[E]ach man concentrates on his immediate convenience," including at most the next generation, easily recognizable flesh and blood (DA, 53). Right here, four pages into Tocqueville's two tomes, two essential themes have been introduced: (a) individualism, the (English) word not yet invented, with its petty retreat into the narrow circle of the immediate family, and (b) the social leveling doing away with a landed aristocracy, not merely "great names and great wealth," but rather a "natural aristocracy of education and probity," preparing one for "a whole life spent publicly, doing good" (DA, 55). No point to castigate Tocqueville for his incorrigible nostalgia for an idealized aristocracy that perhaps never existed. Rather, Tocqueville's first sociotheoretical analysis appears as an inextricable blend of normative, formal and abstract, and localized and interpretive approaches. The interdependence of these three elements in Tocqueville's theoretical practice is clearly illustrated.

And yet, this undeniable interdependence could after all simply be an idiosyncrasy of Tocqueville's working method, hence still entirely fortuitous. For that reason precisely, the theoretical chapters in each part attempted to give a more general logical justification for the combination of the three approaches. In particular, the tables in Chapters 3 and 5 illustrated the complementary relations between formal models and hermeneutics. At least from the viewpoint of applicability and fruitfulness—"truth-value"—the abstract and general explanations reached by the first method complemented the restriction of the latter to local, specific interpretations. Similarly, a hermeneutic inquiry was needed to breathe life into the formal models, provide a value theory, an understanding of the preferences at play in every setting, indeed of the notion of rationality applicable to that specific setting. Unfortunately, when it came to an examination of the methods' "justice-value"—their biases and normative implications—it seemed as if their joined use would only compound the problem. However different the reasons, they both exhibited fatal flaws, in particular a shared relativism of the most extreme kind. Clearly, a well-thought-out normative moment was required to rescue both methods, and Tocqueville's normative stand proved particularly fitted to the task. In short, the three elements of the integrated method needed one another, called for one another theoretically.

Having sufficiently belabored the integral unity of Tocqueville's three-tiered method, the conventional, summary-like part of my conclusion is done. Now, as an effort to conclude this study of Tocqueville's method in a spirit worthy of this inveterate hater of systems (R, 62), the remainder of this conclusion is dedicated to an attack on method, centered on an unforgiving highlighting of its limitations. Roland Barthes has furnished a perfect, self-explanatory motto: "There is nothing more sure to kill research and sweep it off into the leftovers of abandoned works, nothing more sure, than method. At some point one has to turn against method, or at least to treat it without any founding privilege" (1941, 9–10).

Readers having made their way to this point deserve an explanation. I am not about to repudiate all my conclusions, and suddenly turn against the study's central concern. Rather, the following pages should be read as a gloss on Barthes' concluding clause. The aim is to ensure that any claims made on behalf of the methodology discovered remain commensurate with its inherent limitations, till now barely alluded to. Undoubtedly, the advantages and disadvantages of any part of the method have been noted, and resolved through their integration. At stake here, however, are deeper, more intractable flaws.

Unfortunately, the method presented here is not sufficient to guarantee success. The obvious problems are the ever-existing possibilities of abusing a method, however promising it might be, and the elusive intangibles of personal genius, which alone can turn a given method into a gold mine of insights. In all honesty, even a superior gift for perceptiveness offers no guarantees against mistakes, faux pas, and prejudices. In Tocqueville's case, the latter are most evident in his attitude toward the conquered North African natives. And while one can follow the logic pushing a French nationalist afraid of a spreading apathetic individualism to support aggressive colonialism, or the qualms of an advocate of decentralization and local participation in supporting state-run welfare systems, such ultraconservative stands reveal our alleged prophet as a child of his class and time. In these cases, no extended time-horizon saved Tocqueville's analysis from the shortsightedness of most of his contemporary peers. Indeed more advanced views on

Algeria left little mark on Tocqueville, given his systematic, methodical avoidance of other written analyses.

A generalized critique seems in order on this subject. Once one has developed a personal framework, and carried one's own original analysis through, to persist in avoiding the confrontation with other points of view borders on intellectual arrogance. Neutralized as a threat to one's normative stand, and no longer in a position to bias one's analysis, the thoughts and writings of others clearly offer opportunities for crossfertilization, altogether preempted by Tocqueville's aloofness. Rather than completely avoiding any confrontation with other opinions, then, postponing that moment until one's general approach has been determined seems a commendable strategy.

Insofar as this study aimed to understand the longevity and legitimacy of Tocqueville's analyses, the recovery of his methodology falls short from yet another perspective: his special style and cautious language. The distinction between the two is not coincidental. While both contributed enormously to the rise of Tocqueville's massive volumes to the status of bestseller, and still fulfill the same function to some degree, there is much to admire and little to be said about Tocqueville's prose style (White, 1973, discusses his talent as master emplotter). Emulating a style successful a century and a half ago, provided one possesses the required literary craftsmanship, will merely produce a parody unlikely to attract contemporary readers. Tocqueville's hard-won style is ultimately another intangible, part and parcel of his genius. However, there is much to be learned from Tocqueville's general approach to language. To ensure the accessibility of his findings, Tocqueville had to make heavy sacrifices. We have seen how difficult it could be to extract formal models from Tocqueville's discursive presentation: those were mere tools for him. Moreover in that particular case, of course, a principled stand against abstract, formal generalizations furnished part of the explanation. Yet as important was his unshakable commitment to a language accessible to the literate audience, which periodically earned him some learned criticism.

Early on, Raymond Aron compared Tocqueville to Montesquieu in their shared willingness to reach a wide audience even if it meant loosening up or abandoning distinguishing criteria, and forgoing the multiplication of precise, scientific concepts (Aron, 1968, 255). More harshly—and somewhat paradoxically—Melvin Richter indicted Tocqueville for retreating from Montesquieu's pioneering scientific efforts into sloppy, shifty ordinary discourse (Richter, 1970). Of course, one needs only add to these learned commentaries Bourdieu's witty analysis of Montesquieu's sometimes ridiculous "rhetoric of scienticity," especially in expounding his meteorological theory of politics (1982, 227ff), and bring this silly exchange to a close.

On a more serious but also more productive plane, the topic of specialized language was already broached in Chapter 3, in the opening section on formalization. Important distinctions were introduced there, between the hard sciences and the human sciences, and between research and presentation. Around these two an idea of the function and nature of language in social theory can be formulated. Both the specialized technical expertise of the researchers and the mere convenience and speed of the research encourage the development of a shorthand, esoteric jargon. In some sciences, at the edge of our current knowledge, ideas can be communicated solely in that esoteric, if playful language (e.g. larks, quarks, strings, spins). Yet while research in social sciences can be improved greatly through the use of technical tools, bringing along their own bizarre language (e.g. parametric rationality, chicken, J curve, bracketing), it cannot afford to forgo a third step—the translation back into common discourse. Often, powerful concepts will simply carve themselves a place in everyday language: think of some Marxian categories (classes, ideology—in that particular sense and not the older, weaker one), or Freudian concepts (unconscious, sublimation), or even Tocquevillian phrases (tyranny of the majority or, now grossly distorted, individualism). More commonly though, any analysis yielding important results must undergo translation, possibly at the cost of simplification or even vulgarization, back to common discourse. That task can also be important in enabling and encouraging interdisciplinary work or even mere borrowing.

In short, while the hard sciences, even those at the edge of current knowledge, can afford to wait until an eager industrial complex translates their discoveries into tangible practical results, we need to do the work ourselves. More than two millennia ago, Thucydides (II,6) formulated a harsh criterion, usually unattainable, yet perfect as a regulative ideal on this question of language: "One who forms a judgment on any point but cannot explain himself clearly to the people, might have never thought on the subject." While there remains a need and a place, one hopes, for specialized monographs of this kind—which should be accessible across the social sciences, however—our improvements in understanding society, the individual, and their relations must find authors ready to take up Thucydides's challenge.

After all, the discovery that a single method, however successful in the application from which it was reconstructed, would not become the miracle recipe for producing masterpieces in social theory must have surprised no one. More paradoxical, though, is the second limiting claim I propose to defend: Tocqueville's method is not necessary for producing such masterpieces. The achievements of Downs and Olson, of Lévi-Strauss and Foucault, do not lack admirers and followers, despite their methodological narrowness from the ecumenical perspective developed here. Indeed even explicit followers take their liberty with the three moments delineated in this book. A list of such self-professed devotees suffices to indicate the breadth of Tocqueville's methodological legacy—at least before this specific study: compare Dahrendorf's study of German democracy (1967) with Dumont's examination of the Indian caste system (1970a), with Skocpol's comparison of revolutionary struggles (1979). Those last three, however, and others less explicit about their debt, do erase all doubt that only Tocqueville, through the intractable idiosyncrasies of his imagination, designed a three-part methodology of particular robustness. Weber's self-ascribed "dilettantism," Polanyi's historico-econometric studies in political economy, Simmel's quest for lawful regularities of social interaction by way of a hermeneutically informed phenomenological description (for dyadic models first, than triadic, and so on)—all display an admirable (and often, professionally costly) disdain for disciplinary and methodological boundaries.

Is that by-now trendy appeal for interdisciplinarity, and the blurring of genres, all this study has to offer in conclusion? Another claim to fatherhood to add to Tocqueville's already prolifically promiscuous mind? Remember this study's modest beginnings, its initial aim being to recover Tocqueville's methodology, an oddly neglected topic despite the striking longevity of Tocqueville's insights in a rapidly changing world. The three-part structure that emerged from this study, each element first uncovered in a particular text, then detected in Tocqueville's other works, and all three finally synthesized as one integral approach, constituted the answer to that main question. Yet I did harbor a greater ambition, and meant to address a wider audience. I admitted in my introduction a willingness to use Tocqueville as he used America: his ultimate concern was France's political future, and mine the conduct of superior social theory. At this level, the distinction from trendy suggestions for synthesis—as elaborated, in theory, in Donald Moon's essay (1975), to cite one well-known example —lies in two fairly unique characteristics. First, this study reflected a determination to work from the ground up, to recover an already successful "logic of discovery" in practice rather than dictate an a priori methodology, however attractive. Second, the emphasis here was on bridging the most daunting, allegedly insurmountable gaps between what are regarded—

between and *within* disciplines—as irreconcilable approaches: Barry's "economists" and "sociologists," and, perhaps even more unthinkable, Habermas's "classics" and "moderns." In present-day, social-scientific jargon, uniting in any blend the qualifiers "formal," "interpretive," "objective," and "normative" could be but a recipe for an epistemological Molotov cocktail.

One exception, though, immediately comes to mind, and it repays analysis for two reasons. Habermas's impressive accomplishments, attained in complete disregard of "natural" boundaries, inherent disciplinary limits, and other unbridgeable gaps, make him the single most interesting and innovative social scientist today. By that praise no denigration is intended of the many fascinating works and researchers in each field, though a bid for the superiority of Tocqueville's eclectic, ecumenical approach is. However, I also wish to clarify an important distinction between Habermas and Tocqueville—the latter as reconstructed here—on the nature of the third, normative element of their methodology. Habermas's all-too-rigid classification of approaches by their main guiding interest—as though no scientist's quest for (say, medical) nomological laws can ever be emancipatory—dictates a much narrower understanding of the normative moment's character and mode of operation. Bowing to the tradition (even linguistically) of Marx and the contemporary Frankfurt school, Habermas proclaims that the guiding interest must be "emancipatory," specifically guided to a realization by the reader of the structures of domination already implanted within him. At least two dogmatic results flow from this conceptualization: normative means, always and everywhere, critical. Moreover, the theorist must have fully grasped and cleansed herself of those pervasive structures of domination. Habermas is thus led, despite a lengthy exchange of criticisms and self-criticisms, to model the relations between theorist and public on the psychoanalytical encounter (Giddens, 1977, 147, 158), with its strong authoritarian overtones. Tocqueville's "meth-

odology of distance," sustaining a powerful normative commitment while avoiding subjectivism, listing mercilessly the
trade-offs in moral values between alternatives, yet carefully
shying away from offering absolute answers, remains more
open, broader, and much less dogmatic.

Returning to our three-tiered method, in demonstrating that
Tocqueville harbored no hesitation in mixing and shaking all
these elements as his genius perceived the subject dictated,
and consequently for the most part achieving perceptive, long-
lasting insights, one trusts to have cleared a bit of the mutual
paranoia dividing schools and disciplines. Such is the democratic hope at the end of this work. Surely few will ever master
all approaches, in their growing complexity, and instinctively
recognize the blend fitted for the question under consideration.
However, we could all collaborate, in the way any given intractable issue seems to demand, even if our effort begins merely
with a willingness to study each other's contribution—until
we ultimately return to a common language, one which even
our regained audience will understand.

SELECTED BIBLIOGRAPHY

SELECTED BIBLIOGRAPHY

———— ◆•◆ ————

Adorno, Theodor W. *The Jargon of Authenticity*. Evanston, Ill.: Northwestern University Press, 1973(a).

————. *Negative Dialectics*. New York: Seabury Press, 1973(b).

Adorno, Theodor W., et al. *The Positivist Dispute in German Sociology*. London: Heinemann, 1976.

Arendt, Hannah. *The Human Condition*. Chicago: University of Chicago Press, 1958.

Aron, Raymond. "La définition liberale de la liberté," *Archives Européennes de Sociologie*, 2 (1964).

————. *The Main Currents in Sociological Thought*. London: Weidenfeld and Nicolson, 1968.

Attali, Jacques, and Marc Guillaume. *L'anti-économique*. Paris: Presses Universitaires de France, 1975.

Bachrach, Peter. *The Theory of Democratic Elitism: A Critique*. Boston: Little, Brown, 1967.

Barry, Brian. *Sociologists, Economists, and Democracy*. Chicago: University of Chicago Press, 1978.

Barry, Brian, and Douglas W. Rae. "Political Evaluation," in *Handbook of Political Science*, ed. F. I. Greenstein and N. W. Polsby, 1: 337–401. Reading, Mass.: Addison-Wesley, 1975.

Barry, Brian, and Russell Hardin, eds. *Rational Man and Irrational Society?* Beverly Hills: Sage, 1982.

Barthes, Roland. "Ecrivains, intellectuels, professeurs," *Tel Quel*, 47 (1971): 3–18.

Bauman, Zygmunt. *Hermeneutics and Social Science*. New York: Columbia University Press, 1978.

Becker, Carl L. *Detachment and the Writing of History*. Ithaca, N.Y.: Cornell University Press, 1958.

Becker, Gary S. *The Economic Approach to Human Behavior*. Chicago: University of Chicago Press, 1976.

Bendix, Reinhard. *Nation-Building and Citizenship*. New York: Wiley, 1964.

Benjamin, Walter. *Das Passagen-Werk*. Frankfurt: Suhrkamp, 1982.

Berlin, Isaiah. *Four Essays on Liberty*. London: Oxford University Press, 1969.

———. *Russian Thinkers*. New York: Viking Press, 1978.

Bernstein, Richard J. *Beyond Objectivism and Relativism*. Philadelphia: University of Pennsylvania Press, 1983.

Birnbaum, Pierre. *Sociologie de Tocqueville*. Paris: Presses Universitaires de France, 1970.

Bleicher, Josef. *Contemporary Hermeneutics*. London: Routledge and Kegan Paul, 1980.

Boesche, Roger. "Why Could Tocqueville Predict So Well?", *Political Theory*, 11, (1983): 79–97.

Boudon, Raymond. *La logique du social: introduction à l'analyse sociologique*. Paris: Hachette, 1979.

———. *The Crisis in Sociology*. New York: Columbia University Press, 1980.

———. *The Logic of Social Action*. London: Routledge and Kegan Paul, 1981.

———. *The Unintended Consequences of Social Action*. New York: St. Martin's Press, 1982.

———. *La place du désordre*. Paris: Presses Universitaires de France, 1985.

Bourdieu, Pierre. *Esquisse d'une théorie de la pratique*. Geneva: Librairie Droz, 1972.

———. *Ce que parler veut dire*. Paris: Fayard, 1982.

———. *Questions de sociologie*. Paris: Minuit, 1984.

Bradley, Marian, *Nassau Senior and Classical Economics*. New York: Octagon Books, 1967.

Bradley, Phillips. "Introduction" to Alexis de Tocqueville, *Democracy in America*, 1:vii–c. New York: Knopf, 1945.

Brogan, Hugh. "Alexis de Tocqueville: The Making of a Historian," in *Historians in Practice*, ed. W. Laqueur and G. L. Mosse. Beverly Hills: Sage, 1974.

Brown, Richard H. *A Poetic for Sociology*. New York: Cambridge University Press, 1977.

Brown, Robert. *The Nature of Social Laws.* Cambridge, Eng.: Cambridge University Press, 1984.

Brunius, Teddy. *Alexis de Tocqueville: The Sociological Aesthetician.* Uppsala, Sweden: Acta Universitatis Upsaliensis, 1960.

Bryman, Alan. "The Debate About Quantitative and Qualitative Research: A Question of Method or Epistemology?", *British Journal of Sociology,* 35 (1984): 75–92.

Buck, Gunther. "The Structure of Hermeneutic Experience and the Problem of Tradition," *New Literary History,* 10, (1978): 31–49.

Buck, R. C. "Reflexive Prediction," *Philosophy of Science,* 30 (1963), 359–74.

Burke, Peter. *Sociology and History.* London: George Allen & Unwin, 1980.

Cannon, John A., ed. *The Historian at Work.* London: George Allen Unwin, 1980.

Centre National de la Recherche Scientifique. *Alexis de Tocqueville: Livre du centenaire 1859–1959.* Paris: Editions du Centre National de la Recherche Scientifique, 1960.

Cohen, G. A. *Karl Marx's Theory of History: A Defence.* Princeton: Princeton University Press, 1978.

Collingwood, R. G. *The Idea of History,* Oxford: Oxford University Press, 1946.

Collins, Lyndhurst, ed. *The Use of Models in the Social Sciences.* Boulder, Colo.: Westview Press, 1976.

Connolly, William E. *Political Science and Ideology.* New York: Atherton Press, 1967.

Costner, Herbert L. "De Tocqueville on Equality: A Discourse on Intellectual Style," *Pacific Sociological Review,* 19 (1976): 411–29.

Dahrendorf, Ralf. *Society and Democracy in Germany.* New York: Norton, 1967.

Davidson, Donald. *Essays on Actions and Events.* Oxford: Clarendon Press, 1980.

Descombes, Vincent. *Modern French Philosophy.* Cambridge, Eng.: Cambridge University Press, 1980.

Dewey, John. *The Public and Its Problems.* Chicago: Swallow Press, 1954.

Dilthey, Wilhelm. *Gesammelte Schriften.* Stuttgart: Teubner, 1961.

Drescher, Seymour. *Tocqueville and England.* Cambridge, Mass.: Harvard University Press, 1964.

———. *Dilemmas of Democracy: Tocqueville and Modernization.* Pittsburgh: University of Pittsburgh Press, 1968(a).

———. *Tocqueville and Beaumont on Social Reform.* New York: Harper & Row, 1968(b).

Dumont, Louis. *Homo Hierarchicus: An Essay on the Caste System.* Translated by Mark Sainsbury. Chicago: University of Chicago Press, 1970(a).

———. *Religion/Politics and History in India.* Paris: Mouton, 1970(b).

———. *From Mandeville to Marx.* Chicago: University of Chicago Press, 1977.

Durkheim, Émile. *Suicide.* New York: Free Press, 1951.

Eberts, Paul R., and Ronald A. Witton. "Recall from Anecdote: Alexis de Tocqueville and the Morphogenesis of America," *American Sociological Review,* 35 (1970): 1081–97.

Elias, Norbert. *What Is Sociology?* New York: Columbia University Press, 1978.

Elster, Jon. *Logic and Society.* New York: Wiley, 1978.

———. "Anomalies of Rationality: Some Unresolved Problems in the Theory of Rational Behavior," in *Sociological Economics,* ed. Louis Levy-Garbova. Beverly Hills: Sage, 1979.

———. *Explaining Technical Change: A Case Study in the Philosophy of Science.* Cambridge, Eng.: Cambridge University Press, 1983(a).

———. *Sour Grapes.* Cambridge, Eng.: Cambridge University Press, 1983(b).

Ferguson, Adam. *An Essay on the History of Civil Society.* London: Millar and Caddell, 1767.

Furet, François. *Interpreting the French Revolution.* New York: Cambridge University Press, 1981.

———. "Un nouveau paradigme: Tocqueville et le voyage en Amerique," *Annales,* March–April 1984, pp. 225–39.

Gadamer, Hans-Georg. *Philosophical Hermeneutics.* Berkeley: University of California Press, 1977.

———. *Truth and Method.* New York: Crossroad, 1982.

Galbraith, John Kenneth. *The New Industrial State.* 2d ed. Boston: Houghton Mifflin, 1971.

Gargan, Edward T. *Alexis de Tocqueville: The Critical Years 1848–1851.* Washington, D.C.: Catholic University Press, 1955.

———. "Tocqueville and the Problem of Historical Prognosis," *American Historical Review,* 68 (1963): 332–45.

Gay, Peter. *Voltaire's Politics: The Poet as Realist.* Princeton: Princeton University Press, 1959.

Geertz, Clifford. *The Interpretation of Cultures.* New York: Basic Books, 1973.

———. *Local Knowledge.* New York: Basic Books, 1983.

Gellner, Ernest. "Concepts and Society," in *Rationality*, ed. B. Wilson. Oxford: Basil Blackwell, 1970.

———. "The New Idealism—Cause and Meaning in the Social Sciences," in *Positivism and Sociology*, ed. Anthony Giddens. London: Heinemann, 1975.

Giddens, Anthony. *Studies in Social and Political Theory*. New York: Basic Books, 1977.

———. *Profiles and Critiques in Social Theory*. Berkeley: University of California Press, 1982.

———. "Hermeneutics and Social Theory," in *Hermeneutics: Questions and Prospects*, ed. Gary Shapiro and Alan Sica. Amherst: University of Massachusetts Press, 1984.

———, ed. *Positivism and Sociology*. London: Heinemann, 1975.

Goldstein, Doris S. "Alexis de Tocqueville's Concept of Citizenship," *Proceedings of the American Philosophical Society*, 108 (1964).

Gunnell, John G. *Between Philosophy and Politics*. Amherst: University of Massachusetts Press, 1986.

Habermas, Jürgen. *Strukturwandel der Öffentlichkeit*. Neuwied, 1962.

———. *Zur Logik der Sozialwissenschaften*. Special issue of *Philosophische Rundschau*. Tübigen: J. C. B. Mohr, 1967.

———. *Knowledge and Human Interests*. London: Heinemann, 1972.

———. *Theory and Practice*. Boston: Beacon Press, 1973.

Hadari, Saguiv. " 'Persuader sans convaincre': A Rousseauan Approach to the Insoluble Problem of the Social Contract," *Western Political Quarterly*, 39 (1986): 504–19.

———. "What Are Preference Explanations? The Interpretive Core of Economic Modeling," *Social Science Quarterly*, 68 (1987): 340–57.

Hamburger, Henry. *Games as Models of Social Phenomena*. San Francisco: Freeman, 1979.

Hardin, Russell. "Difficulties in the Notion of Economic Rationality," *Social Science Information*, 23 (1984).

Harré, Rom. "The Constructive Role of Models," in *The Use of Models in the Social Sciences*, ed. L. Collins. Boulder, Colo.: Westview Press, 1976.

Hayek, Friedrich A. *Individualism and Economic Order*. Chicago: University of Chicago Press, 1948.

———. *Studies in Philosophy, Politics and Economics*. Chicago: University of Chicago Press, 1967.

Hekman, Susan. *Weber, the Ideal Type and Contemporary Social Theory*. Notre Dame, Ind.: University of Notre Dame Press, 1983.

Henshel, R. L. "The Boundary of the Self-Fulfilling Prophecy and the Dilemma of Social Prediction," *British Journal of Sociology*, 33 (1982): 511–28.

Henshel, R. L., and L. W. Kennedy. "Self-Altering Prophecies: Consequences for the Feasibility of Social Prediction," *General Systems*, 18 (1973): 119–26.

Herr, Richard. *Tocqueville and the Old Regime.* Princeton: Princeton University Press, 1962.

Hersh, Harry M., and Alfonso Caramazza. "A Fuzzy Set Approach to Modifiers and Vagueness in Natural Language," *Journal of Experimental Psychology*, 105 (1976): 254–76.

Hertz, Neil. *The End of the Line.* New York: Columbia University Press, 1985.

Hesse, Mary. *The Structure of Scientific Inference.* London: Macmillan, 1974.

Hindess, Barry. *Philosophy and Methodology in the Social Sciences.* Atlantic Highlands, N.J.: Humanities Press, 1977.

Hirschman, Albert O. *A Bias for Hope.* New Haven, Conn.: Yale University Press, 1971.

Holsti, Ole R. "Theories of Crisis Decision Making," in *Diplomacy: New Approach in History, Theory and Policy*, ed. Paul Gordon Cauren, 99–136. New York: Free Press, 1979.

Hume, David. "That Politics May Be Reduced to a Science," in *Political Essays*, ed. Charles W. Hendel. Indianapolis, Ind. Bobbs-Merrill, 1952.

———. *A Treatise of Human Nature.* Oxford: Clarendon Press, 1978.

Jardin, André. *Alexis de Tocqueville.* Paris: Hachette, 1984.

Jervis, Robert. *Perception and Misperception in International Politics.* Princeton: Princeton University Press, 1976.

Jouvenel, Bertrand de. "Political Science and Prevision," *The American Political Science Review*, 59 (1965): 29–38.

Karitansky, John. "An Interpretation of Tocqueville: Democracy in America." Ph.D. dissertation, University of Chicago, 1970.

Keeney, James. "Tocqueville and the New Politics," *New Politics*, Spring 1982, pp. 58–65.

Kinder, Donald R., and Janet E. Weiss. "In Lieu of Rationality: Psychological Perspectives on Foreign Policy Decision Making," *Journal of Conflict Resolution*, 22 (1978): 707–35.

Koestler, Arthur. *Stranger on the Square.* London: Hutchinson, 1984.

Kolm, Serge-Christophe. "La philosophie bouddhiste et les 'Hommes économiques,'" *Social Science Information*, 18 (1979): 489–588.

Kramer, Gerald H., and Joseph Hertzberg. "Formal Theory," in *Strategies of Inquiry*, ed. F. I. Greenstein and N. W. Polsby, 7: 351–403. Reading, Mass.: Addison-Wesley, 1975.

Lamberti, Jean-Claude. *La notion d'individualisme chez Tocqueville.* Paris: Presses Universitaires de France, 1970.

Laski, Harold. "Alexis de Tocqueville and Democracy," in *The Social and Political Ideas of Some Representative Thinkers of the Victorian Age*, ed. F. J. C. Hearnshaw. New York: Barnes and Noble, 1950.

Lee, Dorothy. *Freedom and Culture*. Englewood Cliffs, N.J.: Prentice-Hall, 1959.

Lefebvre, George. "À propos de Tocqueville," *Annales Historiques de la Revolution Française*, 27 (1955): 313–23.

Leroy, Maxime. *Histoires des idées sociales en France*. Vols. 2 and 3. Paris: Gallimard, 1954, 1962.

Lindblom, Charles. *Politics and Markets*. New York: Basic Books, 1977.

Lipset, Seymour Martin. *The First New Nation*. New York: Basic Books, 1963.

———. *Political Man*. New York: Basic Books, 1968.

Lively, Jack. *The Social and Political Thought of Alexis de Tocqueville*. Oxford: Clarendon Press, 1962.

Lukes, Steven. *Individualism*. Oxford: Basil Blackwell, 1973.

Lyotard, Jean-François. *La condition post-moderne*. Paris: Minuit, 1979.

MacIntyre, Alasdair. "The Idea of a Social Science," in *The Philosophy of Social Explanation*, ed. Alan Ryan. Oxford: Oxford University Press, 1973.

———. *After Virtue*. 2d ed. Notre Dame, Ind.: University of Notre Dame Press, 1984.

Mandeville, Bernard. *The Fable of the Bees*, ed. F. B. Kaye. New York: Oxford University Press, 1924.

Manent, Pierre. *Tocqueville et la nature de la démocratie*. Paris: Juilliard, 1982.

Mannheim, Karl. *Essays in Sociology and Social Psychology*. London: Routledge and Kegan Paul, 1953.

March, James G. "Model Bias in Social Action," *Review of Educational Research*, 42 (1972): 413–29.

———. "Bounded Rationality, Ambiguity, and the Engineering of Choice," *Bell Journal of Economics*, 9 (1978).

March, James G., and Johan P. Olsen. "The New Institutionalism: Organizational Factors in Political Life," *American Political Science Review*, 78 (1984): 734–49.

Marshak, T. A. "On the Study of Taste Changing Policies," *The American Economic Review*, 68 (1978).

May, Ernest R. *Lessons of the Past: The Use and Misuse of History in American Foreign Policy*. New York: Oxford University Press, 1973.

Mayer, J. P. *Alexis de Tocqueville*. New York: Viking Press, 1966.

Menger, Carl. *Untersuchungen über die Methode der Socialwissenschafte und der politischen Ökonomie insbesondere*. Leipzig: Duncker & Humbolt, 1883.

Merton, Robert. "The Unanticipated Consequences of Purposive Social Action," *American Sociological Review*, 1 (1936): 894–904.

——. "The Self-Fulfilling Prophecy," *Antioch Review*, 8 (1948): 193–210.

Mill, John Stuart. "Introductions" to Alexis de Tocqueville, *Democracy in America, Volume I & II*. New York: Schocken Books, 1961.

Moon, J. Donald. "The Logic of Political Inquiry: A Synthesis of Opposed Perspectives," in *Handbook of Political Science*, ed. F. I. Greenstein and N. W. Polsby, 7: 131–228. Reading, Mass.: Addison-Wesley, 1975.

Morton, F. I. "Sexual Equality and the Family in Tocqueville's Democracy in America," *Canadian Journal of Political Science*, 17 (1984): 309–24.

Moulin, Herve. *Game Theory for the Social Sciences*. New York: New York University Press, 1982.

Myrdal, Gunnar. *Objectivity in Social Research*. New York: Pantheon Books, 1969.

Nagel, Ernest. "Problems of Concept and Theory Formation in the Social Sciences," in *Science, Language, and Human Rights*, ed. American Philosophical Association, Eastern Division. Philadelphia: University of Pennsylvania Press, 1952.

Nef, John. "Truth, Belief, and Civilization: Tocqueville and Goblineau," *Review of Politics*, 25 (1963): 460–82.

Nisbet, Robert. *Sociology as an Art Form*. New York: Oxford University Press, 1976.

Noelle-Neumann, Elisabeth. *The Spiral of Silence*. Chicago: University of Chicago Press, 1984.

Olson, Mancur. *The Logic of Collective Action*. Cambridge, Mass.: Harvard University Press, 1965.

Perroux, François. *L'Économie du XXᵉ siècle*. Paris: Presses Universitaires de France, 1969.

Pierson, George Wilson. *Tocqueville in America*. New York: Doubleday, 1959.

Poggi, Gianfranco. *Images of Society: Essays on the Sociological Theories of Tocqueville, Marx, and Durkheim*. Stanford: Stanford University Press, 1972.

Polanyi, Karl. *The Great Transformation*. Boston: Beacon Press, 1944.

Polin, Claude. *Analyse critique "De la démocratie en Amerique"*. Paris: Hatier, 1973.

Popper, Karl. *Conjectures and Refutations*. London: Routledge and Kegan Paul, 1963.

Rabinow, P., and W. M. Sullivan, eds. *Interpretive Social Science: A Reader*. Berkeley: University of California Press, 1979.

Richter, Melvin. "Tocqueville's Contributions to the Theory of Revolution," in *Revolution*, ed. Carl J. Friedrich, 73–121. New York: Atherton Press, 1966.

———. "The Uses of Theory: Tocqueville's Adaptation of Montesquieu," in *Essays in Theory and History*, ed. Melvin Richter, pp. 74–102. Cambridge, Mass.: Harvard University Press, 1970.

———. *Political Theory and Political Education*. Princeton: Princeton University Press, 1982.

Ricoeur, Paul. "The Hermeneutical Function of Distanciation," *Philosophy Today*, 17 (1973): 129–41.

Riesman, David. "Tocqueville as Ethnographer," *American Scholar*, 30 (1961): 174–87.

Rorty, Richard. "The World Well Lost," *Journal of Philosophy*, 69 (1972): 649–65.

Runciman, W. G. *Relative Deprivation and Social Justice*. Berkeley: University of California Press, 1966.

Sainte-Beuve, C-A. *Causeries du Lundi*. Paris: Garnier, 1860.

Salomon, Albert. "Tocqueville, Moralist and Sociologist," *Social Research*, 2 (1935).

———. "Tocqueville's Philosophy of Freedom," *Review of Politics*, 1 (1939): 400–31.

———. "Tocqueville, 1959," *Social Research*, 26 (1959): 449–70.

Santos, E. "Fuzzy Algorithms," *Information and Control*, 17 (1970): 326–39.

Sartre, Jean-Paul. *Critique of Dialectical Reason*. London: NLB, 1976.

Schelling, Thomas C. *Micromotives and Macrobehavior*. New York: Norton, 1978.

Schlaerth, William J. *A Symposium on Alexis de Tocqueville's Democracy in America*. New York: Fordham University Press, 1945.

Schleifer, James T. *The Making of Tocqueville's Democracy in America*. Chapel Hill: University of North Carolina Press, 1980.

Schumpeter, Joseph A. *Capitalism, Socialism, and Democracy*. 3d ed. New York: Harper & Row, 1962.

Sennett, Richard. "Ce que redoutait Tocqueville," *Tel Quel*, 86 (1980): 38–49.

Shapiro, Gary, and Alan Sica. *Hermeneutics: Questions and Prospects*. Amherst: University of Massachusetts Press, 1984.

Shapiro, Michael. *Language and Political Understanding: The Politics of Discursive Practices*. New Haven, Conn.: Yale University Press, 1981.

Sheffrin, Steven. "Habermas, Depoliticization, and Consumer Theory," *Journal of Economic Issues*, 12 (1978).

Simmel, Georg. *On Individuality and Social Forms*, ed. Donald Levine. Chicago: University of Chicago Press, 1971.

Simon, Herbert A. *Administrative Behavior.* New York: Free Press, 1946.
———. *Models of Man.* New York: Wiley, 1957.
———. "From Substantive to Procedural Rationality," in *Philosophy and Economic Theory*, ed. Frank Hahn and Martin Hollis. Oxford: Oxford University Press, 1979.
Simpson, M. C. M. *Correspondence and Conversations of Alexis de Tocqueville with Nassau William Senior, 1834–1859.* New York: Kelley, 1968.
Skocpol, Theda. *States and Social Revolutions.* Cambridge, Eng.: Cambridge University Press, 1979.
Smelser, Neil. "Alexis de Tocqueville as Comparative Analyst," in *Comparative Methods in Sociology*, ed. Ivan Vallier, pp. 19–47. Berkeley: University of California Press, 1971.
Smith, James Bruce. *Politics and Remembrance.* Princeton: Princeton University Press, 1985.
Snyder, P. L., ed. *Detachment and the Writing of History: Essays and Letters of Carl L. Becker.* Ithaca, N.Y.: Cornell University Press, 1958.
Steedman, Ian. "Economic Theory and Intrinsically Non-Autonomous Preferences and Beliefs," *Quaderni*, July 8, 1980, pp. 57–73.
Stinchcombe, Arthur L. *Theoretical Methods in Social History.* New York: Academic Press, 1978.
Stone, John, and Stephen Mennell. *Alexis de Tocqueville on Democracy, Revolution, and Society.* Chicago: University of Chicago Press, 1980.
Stouffer, Samuel, et al. *The American Soldier.* New York: Wiley, 1965.
Strauss, L., and J. Cropsey, eds. *History of Political Philosophy.* Chicago: Rand McNally, 1972.
Taylor, Charles. "Neutrality in Political Science," in *Philosophy, Politics, and Society*, ed. Peter Laslett and W. G. Runciman. Oxford: Basil Blackwell, 1967.
———. "Interpretation and the Sciences of Man," *Review of Metaphysics*, 25 (1971): 5–51.
Taylor, Michael. *Anarchy and Cooperation.* New York: Sage, 1976.
Tocqueville, Alexis de. *Oeuvres complètes*, ed. J. P. Mayer. Paris: Gallimard, 1851.
———. *Nouvelle correspondance entièrement inédite d'Alexis de Tocqueville*, Volume VII of *Oeuvres*, ed. Gustave de Beaumont. Paris, 1866.
———. *Correspondance entre Alexis de Tocqueville et Arthur de Gobineau.* Paris: Plon, 1908.
———. *The Old Regime and the French Revolution.* New York: Doubleday, 1955.
———. *Journey to America.* London: Faber and Faber, 1959.

————. *Democracy in America.* New York: Doubleday, 1969.

————. *Recollections.* London: MacDonald, 1970.

————. *Selected Letters on Politics and Society,* ed. Roger Boesche. Berkeley: University of California Press, 1985.

Tucker, Robert C., ed., *The Marx-Engels Reader.* New York: Norton, 1978.

Ullmann-Margalit, Edna, and Sidney Morgenbesser. "Picking and Choosing," *Social Research,* Winter 1977.

Van Parijs, Philippe. *Evolutionary Explanation in the Social Sciences: An Emerging Paradigm.* Totowa, N.J.: Rowman and Littlefield, 1981.

Vernon, Richard. "Unintended Consequences," *Political Theory,* 7 (1979): 57–74.

Vetterling, M. K. "More on Reflexive Prediction," *Philosophy of Science,* 43 (1976): 278–82.

Veyne, Paul. *Comment on écrit l'histoire suivi de Foucault révolutionne l'histoire.* Paris: Éditions du Seuil, 1978.

von Weizsacker, Carl Christian. "Notes on Endogenous Change of Taste," *Journal of Economic Theory,* 3 (1971).

von Wright, George Henrik. *Practical Reason.* Oxford: Basil Blackwell, 1983.

Walters, Ronald G. "Signs of the Times: Clifford Geertz and Historians," *Social Research,* 47 (1980): 536–56.

Walzer, Michael. *Spheres of Justice.* New York: Basic Books, 1983.

————. *Interpretation and Social Criticism.* Cambridge, Mass.: Harvard University Press, 1987.

Weber, Max. *The Methodology of the Social Sciences.* New York: Free Press, 1949.

Weitman, Sasha R. "The Sociological Thesis of Tocqueville's *The Old Regime and the French Revolution,*" *Social Research,* 33 (1966): 389–406.

White, Hayden. *Metahistory.* Baltimore, Md.: Johns Hopkins University Press, 1973.

————. "The Historical Text as Literary Artifact," in *The Writing of History,* ed. R. H. Canary and H. Kozicki, pp. 41–61. Madison, Wis.: University of Wisconsin Press, 1978.

White, Paul Lambert. "American Manners in 1830," *Yale Review,* 12 (1922): 118–31.

Winch, Peter. *The Idea of a Social Science.* London: Routledge and Kegan Paul, 1958.

————. *Ethics and Action.* London: Routledge and Kegan Paul, 1972.

Wolin, Sheldon. "Political Theory and Political Commentary," in *Political Theory and Political Education,* ed. M. Richter, pp. 190–203. Princeton: Princeton University Press, 1980.

Yaari, Menahem E. "Endogenous Changes in Taste: A Philosophical Discussion," *Erkentniss*, 11 (1977): 157–96.

Yaari, Menahem E., and M. Bar-Hillel. "On Dividing Justly," *Social Choice and Welfare*, 1 (1984): 1–24.

Zadeh, L. A. "Outline of a New Approach to the Analysis of Complex Systems and Decision Processes," *IEEE Transactions on Systems, Man and Cybernetics*, 1973, JMC-3, pp. 28–44.

Zeitlin, Irving M. *Liberty, Equality, and Revolution in Alexis de Tocqueville*. New York: Little, Brown, 1971.

Zeldin, Theodore. *France 1848–1945*. Vol. 1. Oxford: Clarendon Press, 1973.

Zetterbaum, Marvin. *Tocqueville and the Problem of Democracy*. Stanford, Calif.: Stanford University Press, 1967.

————. "Alexis de Tocqueville," in *History of Political Philosophy*, ed. L. Strauss and J. Cropsey. Chicago: Rand McNally, 1972.

INDEX

INDEX

Absolutism, 109–16 *passim*, 124, 127, 136
Action, 15, 44, 46, 56, 92, 97; determinants of, 2; explanation of, 90
Adorno, Theodor, 33, 96
Algeria, 154
America, 2ff, 118–28 *passim*, 157; Americans, 39; role of lawyers in, 115n; Jacksonian, 113, 119
Amos, the Prophet, 145
Ampère, Jean Jacques, 69n
Ancient Regime, 15, 38, 70, 76, 133
Anthropology, 5n, 78f
Archimedean point, 107, 114
Arendt, Hannah, 45
Aristocracy, 36, 72ff, 131, 133f, 151f
Aristotle, 3, 104
Aron, Raymond, 155
Assembly, French, 16, 24

Barry, Brian, 7, 14, 34, 66, 158
Barthes, Roland, 153
Beaumont, Gustave de, 88, 119, 135f
Becker, Carl, 106
Beliefs, 53, 56f, 90, 114, 124
Berlin, Sir Isaiah, 47
Betti, Emilio, 44, 71, 74, 90
Bible, the, 146
Biology, 43n

Birnbaum, Pierre, 106, 114
Bleicher, Josef, 72
Boesche, Roger, 78n, 86, 89ff, 135
Boomerang effect, 18, 22. *See also* Unintended consequences
Boudon, Raymond, 15n, 38, 43, 45, 50, 75; compares Tocqueville with Marx, 55
Bourdieu, Pierre, 55, 80, 139, 143, 155
Brown, Richard, 145ff
Burke, Edmund, 69

Canada, 135
Cannon, John A., 138
Catholicism, 135f
Causal explanation, 6, 44, 80–81, 91f, 95; conservative implications of, 46; relation to morality, 46f, 53; limitations of, 52–59 *passim*, 89
Causality, 19, 43–50 *passim*
Causes, general, 16f, 27f
Centralization, 38, 41; overcentralization, 16; decentralization, 153
Chance, 28f, 48ff, 151. *See also* Prediction
Change, 7, 56, 95, 97
Character, 8, 57
Chemistry, 48
Choice, 47n, 52
Chomsky, Noam, 139

Library of Congress Cataloging-in-Publication Data

Hadari, Saguiv A., 1956–1988.
  Theory in practice: Tocqueville's new science of politics /
Saguiv A. Hadari.
    p. cm.
  Bibliography: p.
  Includes index.
  ISBN 0-8047-1704-4 (alk. paper):
    1. Tocqueville, Alexis de, 1805–1859—Contributions in political
science. I. Title.
  JC229.T8H33 1989   89-30920
  320'.092'4—dc 19   CIP